I

AM

OPENS

OUR EYES

WHY LOOK
HORIZONTALLY
WHEN WE SHOULD BE
LOOKING VERTICALLY?

MANUEL (TREY) CHANEY III

innovo
PUBLISHING

Published by Innovo Publishing, LLC
www.innovopublishing.com
1-888-546-2111

innovo
PUBLISHING

Providing Full-Service Publishing Services for Christian Authors, Artists & Ministries: Books, eBooks, Audiobooks, Music, Film & Courses

I AM OPENS OUR EYES
Why Look Horizontally When We Should Be Looking Vertically?

Library of Congress Control Number: 2019943740
ISBN: 978-1-61314-407-7

Cover Design & Interior Layout: Innovo Publishing, LLC

Printed in the United States of America
U.S. Printing History
First Edition: 2019

"As a teacher and mentor for the Lord Jesus Christ, it is very rewarding to see a student learn about our Lord and then begin to teach others with that knowledge. It is Titus Baptist Seminary's founding scripture verse coming to life (2 Timothy 2:2): 'And the things that thou hast heard of me among many witnesses, the same commit thou to faithful men, who shall be able to teach others also.' Many have learned, but few take it seriously enough to dedicate their lives to the ministry of Jesus Christ. I am very proud of Trey and pray that God will use him mightily as he fights for the Lord's kingdom."

**—Dennis Farr, ThD, President, Titus Baptist Seminary,
LaGrange, GA**

"You get to know someone real good when you watch the way they live their life for a year! Especially under the strict and confining conditions of a federal prison. The overwhelming characteristic of Trey Chaney is an undeniable love for Jesus Christ and for all of God's people. Trey became my friend and brother in Christ while we walked, worked out, ate, prayed, and worshiped together in the Millington federal prison camp from 2016 until 2017. It was an experience that changed my life and brought me closer to my Savior, Jesus Christ. He has the heart of the Apostle Paul and the zeal of the Apostle Peter. I look forward to spending all of eternity with him in our heavenly home, where he will continue to teach me and tell me every day to 'Pick up dat weight.' His discipline and training was much more than physical—it was spiritual in the deepest sense possible. I love him with all my heart, and this book is a true reflection of his heart and experiences from his five years in prison."

**—Larry C. Thornton, President/Executive Producer,
Red Thread Pictures, LLC, Memphis, TN**

"The Bible teaches that we overcome by the blood of the lamb and by the word of our testimony (Rev. 12:11). The blood of the lamb has already been shed. The only thing left is to share our testimony. Many fail to share their testimony because they are ashamed of their test. I'm grateful that this is not the case with Trey Chaney. From a star athlete, to a college graduate, to corporate America, to the penitentiary, to a successful business owner radically changed by Christ—Trey has a story that all need to hear. His story of how God opened his eyes will give you strength and encouragement to know that God can do the same for you no matter where you are and no matter how difficult life is."

**—Dr. Thomas Beavers, Senior Pastor, The Star Church,
Birmingham, AL**

CONTENTS

FOREWORD

The lures of today's world have taken hold of our children's vision through secular attractions. The morals and values that our generation (my and my husband's era) were raised on, and that were proudly displayed as the way to success, are belittled—reduced to little or no value. Those values hold little attraction for the current generation. While technology and social media are the catalysts for our children's advancement intellectually and socially, these are also the strongholds that place them in bondage as well as hinder them from a faith-filled life with Christ. As parents of three children, we have seen firsthand what happens when young people lose their Christ-centered focus and turn their focus to the world.

In this book you will read through the eyes of our only son who was brought up in a faith-based home of Christ. Although he had a Christ-led upbringing, he still faced many worldly challenges. Through those challenges, his vision faltered, he lost sight of Christ, and the consequences of his choices and decisions resulted in him receiving a five-year federal prison sentence. During this wilderness season, our son had time to focus on the true and living God, I Am, who controls vision and sight (which we have been telling him since his first days in the world).

Manuel (Trey) Chaney III, the son of a deacon and a minister, an outstanding athlete and college graduate, and former employee for the government, had all kinds of potential for advancement. Trey is very intelligent and personable. Yet he became caught up in the destructive addictions of today's illusions portrayed through all types of media outlets. These addictions became a lifestyle of lust and greed.

During his period of incarceration, we have seen him depressed, broken, and struggling with a low spirit. As his parents, all we could do during this time was to remain faithful to our God to see him through this season with love and prayers. Because of this love from his parents, sisters, and friends, there is no doubt in our minds why Trey has made a total rehabilitation in his mind, body, and, most of all, in his spirit.

We had the opportunity to see Trey's vision unfold while he was on a furlough from prison for a CrossFit workout and interview for sponsors in December 2016. This is when we saw how God had directly taken control of his life. All of the things Trey has gone through in prison were preparation for the manifestation of God's purpose for his life. We pray that in this book, others will see that life, fortune, and mishaps are unpredictable, but with God, the I AM of this universe, all things are possible.

—Manuel and Bonita Chaney
Father and Mother

PREFACE

Before I formed you in the womb I knew you, before you were born I set you apart. (Jeremiah 1:5 NIV)

It is a wonderful feeling to know that before we even had a conscious thought, our loving Father knew us. Our magnificent God created each one of us uniquely, and He knows our hearts, minds, and bodies completely. He knows each and every step we take, and no matter what we have previously gone through, what we are currently going through, or what we are about to go through, God allowed/allows it to happen for His own divine plan. When we realize that nothing can happen to us in this life without God's hands being in total control, then we can understand that it has to be working out for His grand purpose.

Throughout this book, you will see that God created us to live healthy lives—spiritually, emotionally, mentally, socially, and physically. The Bible tells us, "For the word of the LORD is right and true; he is faithful in all he does" (Psalm 33:4 NIV). If we are to thrive in all the ways He designed us to thrive, we must first believe and trust that everything that God allows to happen in our lives is for our good. "And we know that in all things God works for the good of those who love him, who have been called according to his purpose" (Romans 8:28 NIV). And when we live in this way, He will be most glorified.

There is a concept in life I like to call the "CDC": for every *choice* and *decision* we make, there is a *consequence*. Good or bad, there is a consequence—and we need to be prepared for it. The good thing about all of this is when we trust God, He will make a way when we can't see it. When our bad decisions seem to leave us empty, and we feel like we're drowning, He will open closed doors and unveil new ones. He is a forgiving God who wants to shape us into the disciples

He has created us to be—and He will work together for His good even the bad decisions we make. When we totally submit to God, He will work in our lives for His good and ours.

This book will show, through real life situations, that when all else fails and the worldly "fixes" don't satisfy, the only real choice left to make is for our hearts and minds to trust God completely. He will deliver us from the depths of our sin; He will provide a way for us.

> No temptation has overtaken you except what is common to mankind. And God is faithful; he will not let you be tempted beyond what you can bear. But when you are tempted, he will also provide a way out so that you can endure it. (1 Corinthians 10:13 NIV)

When we are at the end of ourselves, with no one else to turn to, may we look up to find a God who is waiting with His arms stretched wide, waiting for us to run to Him and trust Him with our whole lives.

1

CLOSED EYES

Hear this, you foolish and senseless people, who have eyes but do not see ...
(Jeremiah 5:21 NIV)

V *ision* is defined as something seen by other means than ordinary sight—as in a dream or trance.[1] It is a vivid picture created by the imagination. *Perception* is defined as awareness of one's environment through physical sensation. *Eyesight* is defined as vision or perception.[2]

Many of us live our lives in a hindsight paradigm—"I wish I had done this differently," "I can see now that was the wrong decision," "I never should have done that." We don't see the path we are taking until we have already walked it. The eye is one of the most complex organs in the body, and we have two of them! Yet we live our lives with them closed—like we would rather pay the consequences later rather than stop and think through our choices. This life—light—we are missing by walking with closed eyes, is the world that God created on the first day: "And God said, Let there be light: and there was light. And God saw the light, that it was good" (Genesis 1:3-4 KJV).

Our perfect, holy God created the entire universe in six days. On day one, God created light. Day two, God created firmament. Day three, God created dry land. Day four, He created light bearers.

---

1. Merriam-Webster Dictionary, keyword: *vision*.
2. Merriam-Webster Dictionary, keyword: *eyesight*.

Day five, our God created fish and birds. Day six, the Bible says our God created animals and humans. Lastly, the Bible tells us that God rested. But right before God rested, He decided to take a look at everything He had created. He *saw* it was very good (cf. Genesis 1:31). If our advanced, magnificent, imaginative, perfect Creator was able to create the entire universe but didn't acknowledge its goodness until it was created, then how do we suppose we can see clearly and acknowledge His goodness with our eyes closed?

Our eyes are so unique. The retinas in our eyes separate information into categories—a screening process that keeps the brain from getting overwhelmed by too much visual stimulation. If our eyes are closed, we aren't giving our brains a chance at creation, imagination, or new destinations. A closed eye is also unable to see distance, volume, length, or capacity. With closed eyes, our total metric system is in a moratorium.

We may ask, *How is it possible for our eyes to be open, for us to have 20/20 vision, and yet we still cannot "see"?* The simple answer is we do not trust God with our choices; therefore, we cannot yet see the plan He has in store for us. Although we may see with our eyes, we can't see with our hearts until we give ourselves to Him.

In 2007 I graduated from the University of Alabama Birmingham (UAB). Thinking I had it all figured out, I decided I wanted to purchase a brand-new Cadillac Escalade EXT as a graduation gift to myself. I conjured up this plan to get my father to go with me to the dealership to buy the truck. I remember saying, "Hey, Dad, want to go take a look at some trucks?" With nothing to do on a Saturday, he was overjoyed at spending time with his son. I had already put the down payment in my checking account. I was working two jobs and thought that if I had this truck, I could get all the ladies and be more pleasing to their eyes. My eyelids were open, but my eyes were surely closed.

When we arrived at the dealership, I talked my dad into allowing me to purchase the truck, and I bought my first vehicle off the showroom floor. I failed to mention this truck came with a hefty monthly car payment, insurance premiums through the roof, and a huge gas tank. I was in way over my head. Instead of being able to ride around to see ladies, I was stuck at home with no gas money. The consequence of my poor decision left me in the same situation: I was still struggling with transportation!

My finances were beginning to falter. When I realized later—after I let the truck go—the amount of money I could have saved, I thought of all the other dreams I could have pursued. In hindsight, I knew the foolishness of my choice.

When we totally devote ourselves to trusting God, we do not have to wait on hindsight. God gives us the ability to see things in foresight. Had I just prayed about this decision, God would have guided me in the right direction—no doubt discouraging this purchase. Making a financial decision for the main purpose of impressing women is not a good idea. I found this out the hard way.

Without God's guidance, our eyes are in a state of impotence. There is a creed my family has always lived by: "Closed mouths don't get fed." And closed eyes don't see. Everyone alive today has a view of God—whether it's an exalted view, a stale view, an ignorant view, or a denial view, we make our choices based on our view. If we exalt God with our choices, He is glorified. If we deny God with our choices, He is grieved. We can choose to look to God, or we can choose to continue living life with closed eyes, denying His presence in our lives.

God gives us eyes to look toward Him—vertically. If we are looking elsewhere—horizontally—we have no one else to blame for our circumstances but ourselves.

I love the poem by Mayme W. Miller called "Yourself to Blame":

> If things go bad for you
> And make you a bit ashamed
> Often you will find out that
> You have yourself to blame
>
> Swiftly we ran to mischief
> And then the bad luck came
> Why do we fault others?
> We have ourselves to blame
>
> Whatever happens to us,
> Here is what we say
> "Had it not been for so-and-so
> Things wouldn't have gone that way"

And if you are short of friends,
I'll tell you what to do
Make an examination,
You'll find the faults in you . . .

You're the captain of your ship,
So agree with the same
If you travel downward
You have yourself to blame[3]

It's understandable why we have closed eyes because of the era of narcissistic entitlement we live in today. When our eyes are closed off to God, all we do is elevate ourselves. We are self-centered and constantly comparing ourselves with others, and we believe we are entitled to what others have—not to mention, we often believe we deserve more than others.

For what is a man profited, if he shall gain the whole world, and lose his own soul? or what shall a man give in exchange for his soul? (Matthew 16:26 KJV)

Without God, our eyes will remain closed. We will continue to go about in this self-obsessed era, believing we should be entitled to whatever little selfish concern we harbor. In other words, what good does it do to have all the temporary things of this world and miss out on the eternal things of everlasting life? At some point in our lives, we will have to at least peek through our eyelids, stop caring about attracting millions of followers for ourselves, and truly commit to following Christ.

On the Day of Judgment, it will not matter if your username attracted millions of followers; it will matter if your true name is printed in the Lamb's Book of Life. It is time we open our closed eyes!

---

3. This poem by Mayme W. Miller was taken from *Think Big* by Ben Carson. Copyright © 2009 by Ben Carson. Used by permission of Zondervan. www.zondervan.com.

2

BLURRED VISION

For if a man think himself to be something, when he is nothing, he deceiveth himself. (Galatians 6:3 KJV)

A *blur* is defined as something "vaguely perceived" or "a smear or stain that obscures."[4]

There is a vast difference between *knowing about* God and truly *knowing* God. Many of us simply know about God. We may know God through our parents, teachers, pastors, or other means. For most of our lives, we have heard the stories of the Bible. We have sat through many a sermon. But what makes us true believers is that we know God and are saved through faith in Him.

We must experience and discover a procedure before we actually understand it. We can usually walk before we can define walking or talk before we can define talking. Most of us don't learn how to define terms until we are in school—and most of us never learn how to do that well. In general, activity precedes definition.[5]

Likewise, many regular church attenders simply go through the motions of knowing *about* God, not actually understanding the path to true knowledge of Him. They don't put in the effort to experience and discover God and His work in their lives. They don't

---

4. Merriam-Webster Dictionary, keyword: *blur.*

5. John M. Frame, *Salvation Belongs to the Lord: An Introduction to Systematic Theology* (Philipsburg, NJ: P&R Publishing Company, 2001).

truly understand who He is, and they live their lives (for the most part) ignorant of it. This is *blurred vision.*

> *Not every one that saith unto me, Lord, Lord, shall enter into the kingdom of heaven; but he that doeth the will of my Father which is in heaven. (Matthew 7:21 KJV)*

I find it interesting to hear people in long-term relationships say during times of disagreement, "You do not understand me." In retrospect, this statement is partially true. Blurred vision is the catalyst that presses us towards desires of the flesh—not taking the time to understand each other because all we desire is instant gratification. It is no wonder the majority of women are attracted to a six-foot tall, athletically built man with a seven-hundred credit score and a nice car. It is not surprising that men lust after a woman wearing revealing, attractive clothes, with long hair and six-inch heels. This is what the world has taught us to be attracted to. Everywhere we look—from social media to television—sexual appeal is being blasted into our eyes, causing our vision to be blurred.

So not only are our eyes blurred to true knowledge of our Creator, but they are blurred to the world around us as well. We must take time to understand God's view of us if we desire to retract the blurred vision the world has taught us to have.

> *But the LORD said unto Samuel, Look not on his countenance, or on the height of his stature; because I have refused him: for the LORD seeth not as man seeth; for man looketh on the outward appearance, but the LORD looketh on the heart. (1 Samuel 16:7 KJV)*

I remember when I was in college, and I saw this young lady in one of my classes. I thought to myself, *She is the hottest woman I have ever seen.* I started to scroll through her social media accounts. Social media is a platform, to my understanding, where we can put details about ourselves for the world to see. The issue with this is most people simply put out their best details. While I was "researching" this young lady, I noticed that everything about her was just what I wanted—a gorgeous smile, attractive body, and long hair. In my blurred vision, she was fine as wine!

When I finally asked her out and we began dating, my mind was set on satisfying my flesh, and hers was set on satisfying her bank accounts. In the end, both of us became insatiable. We were only together to satisfy our selfish needs, which ultimately led to the end of our relationship.

When our vision is blurred, we think we have found what we are searching for because of the outward appearance. When we look introspectively at a person or a situation, more times than not we will acquire a clearer picture of what we are really looking for.

> *Anyone who listens to the word but does not do what it says is like someone who looks at his face in a mirror and, after looking at himself, goes away and immediately forgets what he looks like. (James 1:23-24 NIV)*

Blurred vision compels us to deceive ourselves if we think merely being exposed to Christian ministry and biblical teaching is enough to keep us in a right relationship with God. We can be involved in all kinds of church activity and ministry and know a lot about God's Word, but if we do not put that Word into practice, all of our activity and knowledge is meaningless.[6] What good does it do to read the Word of God but then go our way without responding to what it revealed about our lives? The fact is, we truly learn and retain things only as we put them into practice.[7] Until we truly learn to activate our eyesight for the Lord, then our vision will remain blurred.

> *Where there is no vision, the people perish. (Proverbs 29:18 KJV)*

When we do not have a clear and inspired vision for following God's plan, we likely lack spiritual passion and conviction. When we allow blurred vision to guide us, we succumb to the ways of the world. In that moment, the worldly behaviors, lifestyles, and beliefs lead us. This is totally contrary to God's Word.

---

6. *Fire Bible*, James 1:22 note. (Springfield, MO: Life Publishers International, 1984).

7. *Fire Bible*, James 1:24 note.

Let your eyes look straight ahead; fix your gaze directly before you. Give careful thought to the paths for your feet and be steadfast in all your ways. Do not turn to the right or the left; keep your foot from evil. (Proverbs 4:25-27 NIV)

We have to find ways to clear the smear or stain that obscures our vision of what God's Word has set before us. If we want to live up to our God-given potential, we have to clear our eyes of the world's blurred vision.

3

EYEGLASSES

So that we ourselves glory in you in the churches of God for your patience and faith in all your persecutions and tribulations that ye endure. (2 Thessalonians 1:4 KJV)

E *yeglasses* are defined as "lenses worn to aid vision."[8] Remember in chapter one, we defined *vision* as something seen otherwise than by ordinary sight—a vivid picture created by the imagination. In a way, vision is closely related to having faith. They both begin with a hopeful, desired spiritual thought before they manifest physically. The Bible says, "Now faith is the substance of things hoped for, the evidence of things not seen" (Hebrews 11:1 KJV). This means that our vision or faith (VF: *vision faith*) is not based on visible circumstances, but our VF is based on the evidence in the Spirit.

The concept behind this type of inspection is to put on our eyeglasses. When we put on our eyeglasses, we begin to give aid to our VF. We need something that will aid us as we look to God and not to worldly quick fixes. This aid we are looking for is something that could change our lives forever. This VF aid is simply this: patience. The Bible speaks about patience in many verses. One verse of note is found in James: "But let patience have her perfect work, that ye may be perfect and entire, wanting nothing" (James 1:4 KJV).

---

8. Merriam-Webster Dictionary, keyword: *eyeglasses*.

This assessment James gives us about our eyeglasses of patience is of great adulation. When we start to use our VF aid, patience, we begin to become complete, wanting for nothing. *Patience* is defined as "bearing pain or trials without complaint," showing self-control.[9] In other words, these eyeglasses can be the catalyst for us to withstand and persevere.

I remember when I was working for the YMCA Youth Center in Birmingham, Alabama. I had just received a seasonal promotion as an aquatics supervisor. I was making more money than I had ever made. I spoke with my mom about me getting a credit card to help establish my credit. I wanted to be able to buy certain things! One credit card should be manageable, I thought.

My mom said, "Trey, you don't need any credit cards. Just be patient, and wait on your check every two weeks."

I wasn't interested in hearing that. My eyes were closed, and when I did open my eyes, all I could see was trying to appeal to the ladies.

Eventually I applied for a credit card anyway. When I was approved, they gave me a $10,000 credit limit. My plan was only to use a little, but I used the whole credit limit in just one month. I just couldn't control myself. I kept swiping that card for two months, until . . . my mother discovered my habit. I will never forget her reaction when she opened my credit card bill. I can still hear her frantic call in my head when she means business: *"Trey! Trey!"*

My startled, frightened reply was, "Ye, yes ma'am."

"Get up here!" she yelled.

I dashed up the stairs to where the yelling was coming from.

"I know you didn't spend no $10,000 on no credit card in two months."

Under my breath, I responded, "I didn't mean to. It just happened."

"And what crazy credit card company gives a nineteen-year-old who works at a pool a $10,000 spending limit?" she said. Before I could respond, she said, "Well, I tell you what, I ain't paying it! You gonna pay it, and I'm telling ya' daddy, and he ain't gonna pay it either. Get out!"

As I walked away from her room, I thought, *How you gonna kick me out your room, and you called me to come in?*

---

9. Merriam-Webster Dictionary, keyword: *patience.*

I picked up a second job at night at a stocking company and cut grass all summer in order to make the money to pay back my debt. Working so hard and long (instead of spending time with friends and vacationing) taught me I should have taken Mom's advice in the first place: "Just be patient."

> *And not only so, but we glory in tribulations also: knowing that tribulation worketh patience; And patience, experience; and experience, hope. (Romans 5:3-4 KJV)*

This verse from Romans reminds me of a story of a prophet I like to read about in times when I don't understand something. When I need to put on my eyeglasses of patience, I turn to Habakkuk. He was a prophet during a troubling time for Judah. He wanted to understand what actions God was going to take against His sinful people. Habakkuk didn't understand how God was going to use an even more wicked people to punish His own people. Eventually God assured Habakkuk that He would deal with all wickedness in the right time and way. In the meantime, the righteous folks in Judah would have to pull out their eyeglasses of patience and live by faith (Habakkuk 2:4).

In Habakkuk 2, God gave Habakkuk an answer to his questions about why evil seemed to dominate the world and why He would allow those who do good and right to be wiped out.[10]

> *And the LORD answered me, and said, Write the vision, and make it plain upon tables, that he may run that readeth it. For the vision is yet for an appointed time, but at the end it shall speak, and not lie: though it tarry, wait for it; because it will surely come, it will not tarry. (Habakkuk 2:2-3 KJV)*

God's answer to Habakkuk was a statement that revealed that even though some things seem to take a long time, we just have to simply wait. Pull out our eyeglasses of patience, put faith in God, and just wait.

Let me be the first to tell you, if you haven't heard:

> *Hast thou not known? hast thou not heard, that the everlasting God, the LORD, the Creator of the ends of the earth, fainteth*

---

10. *Fire Bible*, Habakkuk 2:2-20 note.

not, neither is weary? there is no searching of his understanding. He giveth power to the faint; and to them that have no might he increaseth strength. Even the youths shall faint and be weary, and the young men shall utterly fall: But they that wait upon the LORD shall renew their strength; they shall mount up with wings as eagles; they shall run, and not be weary; and they shall walk, and not faint. (Isaiah 40:28-31 KJV)

To wait upon the Lord or to put on your eyeglasses of patience means we have to trust Him completely with our lives. We have to wait patiently for His promises and purposes to be fulfilled. God promises that if we will patiently trust Him, He will provide whatever we need.

Trust in the LORD with all thine heart; and lean not unto thine own understanding. In all thy ways acknowledge him, and he shall direct thy paths. (Proverbs 3:5-6 KJV)

4

EYE STRESSES AND STRAINS

When I heard, my belly trembled; my lips quivered at the voice: rottenness entered into my bones, and I trembled in myself, that I might rest in the day of trouble. (Habakkuk 3:16 KJV)

A *strain* is defined as excessive tension or exertion (as of body or mind). An *eye strain* is defined as a "weariness or strained state of the eye."[11]

This preoccupied lifestyle we live leaves us in a prefabricated state of obduracy. God has created us an intricate body to withstand many forces that come against it here on earth. If we continue enduring these stresses and strains in our lives, this rigorous lifestyle can become intransient. Whether or not we know it or want to admit it, we cannot solve these issues ourselves. Much of the time sin is the cause for the majority of our stresses and strains. Sin does three things in our lives. Sin takes us farther than we want to go. Sin keeps us longer than we want to stay. Also, sin costs us more than we want to pay. Even though we know the consequences of our sins, we continue in them all the same. So, Paul says in Romans 1:32 that even though the wicked know that they who sin are worthy of death,

---

11. Merriam-Webster Dictionary, keyword: *strains; eye strain.*

they go on sinning anyway. "As we can see that sin affects not only our behavior, but our intellect as well."[12]

Sin may be the cause of most stresses and strains. As we know, sin is deserving of death—the first sin is what brought about our mortality in the first place. Therefore, with any sinful choice we make, we should expect some sort of consequence.

We have all heard the saying, "Stress will kill ya." Stresses and strains on us can make us feel exhausted, overwhelmed, hopeless, and pained. These stresses can come in the form of rebellious children, a lost job, financial hardships, or even infidelity. These hardships *will* take a toll on us—maybe not to the extent of killing us, but they are difficult nonetheless.

There are many irregularities our bodies go through when dealing with these types of stressors. Our muscles tense up, especially in our face, neck, and shoulders, leaving us with back or neck pain or painful headaches. We may feel tightness in our chest, a pounding pulse, or muscle cramps. We may even experience problems such as insomnia, heartburn, stomachache, diarrhea, or frequent urination. The worry and discomfort of all these physical symptoms can, in turn, lead to even more stress, creating a vicious cycle between our mind and body.[13]

Now the question is, how do we prevent these stresses and strains? It is nearly impossible to stop hardships from happening in our lives, but there is something we can do to alleviate the pain. When stressful situations arise in our lives, we must stop trying to fix the issues on our own. We must simply seek out a place of rest. The safest place of rest is in God's hands. Jesus says that He will give us rest if we just come to Him (Matthew 11:28).

Jesus' gracious invitation is extended to all of us dealing with stresses and strains, which are the result of the troubles of life and the sins of our human nature. By coming to Jesus for forgiveness and help, and by committing our lives to Christ and following His direction, we find rest and relief from misfortunes.

---

12. John M. Frame, *Salvation Belongs to the Lord* (Phillipsburg, NJ: P&R Publishing Company, 2006) Chapter 8, "Sin and Evil."

13. Lawrence Robinson, Jeanne Segal, Ph.D., Melinda Smith, M.A., "The Mental Health Benefits of Exercise," *HelpGuide.org*, (June 2019). https://www. helpguide.org/articles/healthy-living/the-mental-health-benefits-of-exercise.htm

Come unto me, all ye that labour and are heavy laden, and I will give you rest. Take my yoke upon you, and learn of me; for I am meek and lowly in heart: and ye shall find rest unto your souls. For my yoke is easy, and my burden is light. (Matthew 11:28-30 KJV)

This brings to mind the stressful, straining situation I was dealing with before I was sentenced to seventy months in prison as a result of my sins. I will never forget the day I was arrested for the crimes I committed while working for the government. It was November 9, 2010. I was sitting at my desk when a federal agent walked over and told me she needed me to step away from my desk. She then began to read me my rights and asked me to ride with her and their team to my home while they searched my home and businesses.

From that day until I surrendered myself to prison, my life was in a downward spiral from the poor choices and decisions I had made. I began to use drugs, drink heavily, and engage promiscuously with numerous women. I gained weight. I lost my job. I suffered from sickness and was in and out of the hospital. The worst part: I lost my fiancée, the woman I had planned to spend the rest of my life with.

During this time, my spirit was burdened. My stressful and straining situation drove me into depression. I was diagnosed with Bell's palsy, a condition marked by paralysis of the face, known to be brought on by stressful or straining situations. I was hospitalized because of stress, and I began to drink heavily and abuse drugs. I was in a heinously difficult position.

One Sunday morning at church, I heard my pastor say, "Stop trying to hold on to all this stress and strain. We have to let it all go. We have to let go and let God." This statement changed my view on the hardships I was going through. I finally shrugged my shoulders and decided I needed to give it all—my sickness, depression, relationships, job, money—everything—to God.

But now the LORD my God has given me rest on every side, and there is no adversary or disaster. (1 Kings 5:4 NIV)

Only God can give us complete rest from the stresses and strains of life. In the book *Atlas Shrugged* by Ayn Rand, the objectivist philosopher writes,

> If you saw Atlas the giant who holds the world on his shoulders, if I saw that he stood, blood running down his chest, his knees buckling, his arms trembling, but still trying to hold the world aloft, with the last of his strength, and the greater his effort the heavier the world bore down upon his shoulders, what would I tell him to do? Tell him to shrug.[14]

God didn't design us to bear the weight of the world. God designed us to do our best and allow Him to do the rest.

> *There remains, then, a Sabbath-rest for the people of God; for anyone who enters God's rest also rests from their works, just as God did from his. Let us, therefore, make every effort to enter that rest, so that no one will perish by following their example of disobedience. (Hebrews 4:9-11 NIV)*

We need a place of rest during times of stresses and strains. Just like when my late grandmother, Rose Chaney, would close her eyes, as if sleeping after a long day. I would ask, "Ma' Dear, you sleep?" She would respond, "Nah, Baby, I'm just resting my eyes with the Lord." We must find a place of rest with the Lord too.

---

14. Ayn Rand, *Atlas Shrugged* (New York: Random House, 1957).

5

BLINDFOLDED

And in that day shall the deaf hear the words of the book, and the eyes of the blind shall see out of obscurity, and out of darkness. (Isaiah 29:18 KJV)

B *lindfold* is defined: "to cover the eyes with or as if with a bandage."[15]

Why do we often look to people before we look to God for guidance? A better question is, why do we look to the creation before we look to the Creator? In situations when we are blindfolded, most of the time the one who blindfolded us is another person, a group of people, and/or society. And usually the ones blindfolding us are the ones closest to us.

Throughout much of our adolescence, we have been taught to conform to the surrounding customs. From the time we were born, we have been given instructions on how it is better to work with others than by ourselves. *Two heads are better than one,* they say. In a sense, these are well-intentioned practices. We have all resolved a problem while working with others. The majority of us, at some point in our lives, have received advice from a friend or loved one. We are surrounded by advice and opinions.

But the collection of all these ideologies places us at a spiritual disadvantage. These ideologies compel us to seek man, not just the new fads or trends. This process creates the blindfold idealism (BFI).

---

15. Merriam-Webster Dictionary, keyword: *blindfold*.

When we allow BFI to overtake us, we lose strength in our spiritual walk with God.

God wants us to come to Him first with our every want or need. Our perfect God is omniscient. This means our God has infinite awareness, understanding, and insight about everything that happens in our lives. Who would not want perfect, all-knowing guidance from such a God?

In many situations, we could limit much of our time that is spent searching for a solution to our problems by seeking God first. Instead, we go to everyone and anywhere else first to get the assistance we need. It seems more tangible to us. Then, when that well runs dry, and we have no one else to call, we turn to God. Our BFI keeps us spiritually blind and unable to hear from God.

Does God like us to come to Him after we have tried everything else? God does not want to be our second or third choice. God does not want to be our friend only when we need something. How would you feel if a friend came to you for advice, and you later found out you were the third or fourth person he came to? God wants to be our best friend—our Father—every day and in every way. God wants to hear our most difficult questions so He can give us the answers we seek.

Many times when we ask God first, He sends the answer through the mouths or actions of others. Christ knows and is moved with compassion by our weaknesses, and He is able to relate to all we experience in life. Therefore we can confidently approach God, knowing that our prayers are welcomed and desired by Him.[16] God says in His Word,

> *Let us then approach God's throne of grace with confidence, so that we may receive mercy and find grace to help us in our time of need. (Hebrews 4:16 NIV)*

God gives us answers to our questions when we come to Him first. It may not be the answers we want, and He may give them in a different way than we'd planned, but He wants us to ask Him first. When we do, we can call this God's "indications of direction to our hard questions." He will give us direction through difficult situations—but we need to *ask*.

---

16. *Fire Bible*, Hebrews 4:16 note.

This is how we know that we belong to the truth and how we set our hearts at rest in his presence: If our hearts condemn us, we know that God is greater than our hearts, and he knows everything. Dear friends, if our hearts do not condemn us, we have confidence before God and receive from him anything we ask, because we keep his commands and do what pleases him. And this is his command: to believe in the name of his Son, Jesus Christ, and to love one another as he commanded us. The one who keeps God's commands lives in him, and he in them. And this is how we know that he lives in us: We know it by the Spirit he gave us. (1 John 3:19-24 NIV)

This verse can be summarized by something a friend of mine, Larry "Thunder" Thornton, always says, "It's simple: we ask God first, and we have a peace and confidence, or we have a condemned heart and no peace and no confidence."

There was a time after my indictment where I was struggling financially. All my life I had been taught to "never let them see you down" and that "a man should be able to stand on his own two feet, ten toes down." These thoughts thrust me into believing I could do it on my own if I just worked harder. In my mind, I was blindfolded by what I had been taught my whole life. The premise I believed was if I couldn't make a way, then I would seek guidance from someone else. The problem is, because of my pride, I didn't want to go to my parents or loved ones for help. Like most of us, I went to someone else for help.

During this time period, I was the owner of Tmanic Recording Studios. It had become a pretty popular recording studio in Birmingham, Alabama. I knew that many of the aspiring rappers who recorded in my studio were in the drug game. I decided to speak with one of them about plugging me in (helping me to get the drugs to sell).

One night after Ray[17] finished his recording session, I said, "Bruh, I need you to put me on."

Ray responded, "Man, for real? With you owning the studio, we can lock down the whole city."

In my mind, I was not trying to lock down the city, I just wanted to pay my bills.

---

17. Name has been changed to protect the privacy of the individual.

Later that day, Ray fronted me with five, 120-count pill bottles of Lortabs and a quarter pound of what we called "loud" (marijuana). I was getting the bottles for $150 and selling them for $300. I would also take twenty pills out of each bottle and make a sixth bottle. I remember saying to Ray, "I can get off these pills easier," so I gave the "loud" back. For my $750, I was making a $1,050 profit.

I'll never forget the elation I felt to be back on again—I was making money, and I felt the thrill of success. The problem with this blindfold was that it kept me looking to myself and others and not seeking God. That's just what the devil wanted. These blindfolds kept my focus sideways—horizontal—rather than vertical.

Ironically, this type of view was only a temporary fix for my situation. My plug ended up running out of the products, and I was back in the same predicament. If I had just sought God first, He would have pointed me in the right direction from the start of my dilemma. God doesn't give temporary relief; God offers a permanent solution. Deuteronomy 33:27 (KJV) says, "The eternal God is thy refuge, and underneath are the everlasting arms."

When we are blindfolded by our old ways of thinking, and when the patterns of teaching we have accumulated from people and our society over time leave our eyes covered, we need to seek God's glory and not our own or others'. We need to take the blindfold off and look God straight in the face. He will give us the strength that we need to get through. The Bible says, "So do not fear, for I am with you; do not be dismayed, for I am your God. I will strengthen you and help you; I will uphold you with my righteous right hand" (Isaiah 41:10 NIV).

We just have to seek God first before we take another step. Pray first, move second—this is a phrase I say to guys all the time. We can rest assured, knowing our God will provide when we seek Him first.

But seek ye first the kingdom of God, and his righteousness; and all these things shall be added unto you. (Matthew 6:33 KJV)

"Men have been taught that it is a virtue to stand together,"[18] when the Creator is waiting for us to stand with Him first.

---

18. Ayn Rand, *Atlas Shrugged.*

6

BLINDED

There is a generation that are pure in their own eyes, and yet is not washed from their filthiness. (Proverbs 30:12 KJV)

B *linded* is defined as lacking or grossly deficient in ability to see.[19] Because blindness is the most complicated of all the subjects in this book, we will separate the sexes to understand this subject more in depth. This is not to condemn either party but to bring more awareness to both male and female perspective.

MALE

With media of all forms pouring the non-biblical phrase "cash is king" into our minds, it is no wonder we are aroused at the pursuit of happiness by having more. Men seek to get more and more by any means necessary—more money, more material goods, more women. The media is the primary culprit for cultivating men's fleshly desires as well. It provides an outlet for "escape" into a world of fantasy. But the media cannot be blamed. We are responsible for our own thoughts and actions.

We feel the need to conform to broken paradigms of behavior. The patriarchs of our neighborhoods and societies lead us into thinking that having more money and more women bestows upon

---

19. Merriam-Webster Dictionary, keyword: *blind.*

us our manhood and results in a happy life. Society and technology make it very easy to think we can have anything our flesh desires. We feed our minds filth, and then we expect to find lasting happiness. We fuel our systems with reality TV, blinding ourselves to the reality we live in.

Pornography and lust have become ubiquitous in our world. They are so prevalent that we don't even have to work hard to find them—they're on TV, in print media, at the mall, in the grocery store. But the temporary satisfaction man receives by succumbing to these temptations is doing more harm than he may realize. How can you expect to be a loving, committed husband when you've filled your mind with images of worldly happiness rather than how God designed marriage to be—two individuals with eyes only for each other, no judgment or comparison . . . true, boundless, trustworthy love. But marriage is on the decline, worldwide. In fact, "Across the globe, increasing numbers of women and men are not simply postponing marriage but forgoing it altogether. Among women in their late 30s or early 40s, 29 percent are unmarried in Denmark; 18 percent in Italy; 22 percent in Lebanon; and 32 percent in Libya."[20] This is not how God intended it to be.

For the first time in American history, a majority of adults now live outside of marriage—as single parents, as partners in a cohabitating relationship, or as singles. We aren't doing marriage right.

Some believe having more money is the driving force behind feeding our fleshly desires; the more money we have, the more happiness our flesh can acquire. But the problem is not money. Having money does not make us good or bad. What we do with that money shows where our heart is. As a character in the book *Atlas Shrugged* says,

> Money is only a tool, it will take me wherever I wish, but will not replace me as the driver. It will give me the means for satisfaction of my desires, but it will not provide me with desires. Money will not purchase

---

20. Steven Mintz, Ph.D., "Is Marriage in Decline?" *PsychologyToday.com*, 2015. https://www.psychologytoday.com/us/blog/the-prime-life/201503/is-marriage-in-decline

happiness for a man who has no concept of what he wants.[21]

The problem is, men do not truly understand our purpose in society. We are taught that if we work hard, we can make enough money to buy our happiness—to satisfy our desires. But we have a blinded view on what we *should* desire. The Bible speaks candidly about loving money:

> *For the love of money is the root of all evil: which while some coveted after, they have erred from the faith, and pierced themselves through with many sorrows. (1 Timothy 6:10 KJV)*

What I haven't mentioned yet is that as I write this, I am sitting in federal prison. When I think back to what brought me here, I realize it was my very own blinded vision for the love of money. My entire life I had been a stand-up, honest fellow, until I began to fall into the blindness of the love of money. I began thinking of ways I could get my hands on more money to buy more stuff so I could be pleasing to the eyes of women and ultimately make myself happier. I thought that having more money would give me a position of power among my peers.

This blinded viewpoint is what led to the scheme I created at my government job. I decided to access recently dormant bank accounts of deceased people in order to drain the funds. I figured the bank would eventually close the account and claim the money, so I thought I would beat them to it. For nearly ten months, I spent my days running up my credit cards and paying them off with multiple bank accounts that weren't my own. Eventually I was caught in my scheme.

As I reflect on what led me to make these poor decisions, it was never money, women, or material possessions; rather, it was my blinded view of my purpose as a man. There were many insecurities I had as a young man, but none compared to the "identity" confusion I had. One day I wanted to be a faithful husband, father, and family man, and the next day I wanted power, influence, and celebrity status for all the wrong reasons. My misguided conceptions came from everything I was feeding my mind—television, the internet, and,

---

21. Ayn Rand, *Atlas Shrugged*.

most of all, social media. I was ostentatious and narcissistic, and I believed I was a full-grown man.

Society gave me a faulty view of how a real man should look, act, and think, which drove me to this façade. I have always believed in Christ, and I was saved, but I never wholeheartedly practiced living a life of Christ until I got to prison. I then realized that the only way to have purpose and fulfillment was to pursue the will of Christ for my life.

> *These are the things you are to teach and insist on. If anyone teaches otherwise and does not agree to the sound instruction of our Lord Jesus Christ and to godly teaching, they are conceited and understand nothing. They have an unhealthy interest in controversies and quarrels about words that result in envy, strife, malicious talk, evil suspicions and constant friction between people of corrupt mind, who have been robbed of the truth and who think that godliness is a means to financial gain. But godliness with contentment is great gain. For we brought nothing into the world, and we can take nothing out of it. But if we have food and clothing, we will be content with that. Those who want to get rich fall into temptation and a trap and into many foolish and harmful desires that plunge people into ruin and destruction. (1 Timothy 6:2-9 NIV)*

These verses finally gave me clarity on what I was to pursue as well as what would give me fulfillment. Godliness with contentment gave me the most remarkable feeling, which was the inspiration for a song I wrote called "Simple Things":

Chorus

Don't want no big houses, no big rings,
I just want them simple things.
You can keep them big whips and them long chains,
I just want them simple things.

Verses

You can keep the 40 acres and the mule,
All I ever wanna do is be free with my dudes.

Gotta old lady on my side and she's been ridin',
Holding hands in public, yeah that simple stuff exciting.
Yeah!

Are you club hopping, you club hopping, you club
hopping, you club hopping?
When I step on the scene boy, all I'll be is club dodging.
People in my past, yeah, they callin' me lame,
But what they don't know is prison done made me love
simple things.

I just wanna be me, and you can be the man.
They given more time for the one that's orchestrating
the plan.
When I get back home you can call me a square,
But one thing's for sure, I'll be breathing free air.[22]

I figured out that only through God could I be fulfilled, and
He is the only way to replace the identity confusion I was having. I
learned in His Word that the only way to achieve fulfillment in Christ
was to let go of the old, worldly way of thinking and cling to His
way.

> *But you, man of God, flee from all this, and pursue righteousness,
> godliness, faith, love, endurance and gentleness. Fight the good
> fight of the faith. Take hold of the eternal life to which you were
> called when you made your good confession in the presence of
> many witnesses. In the sight of God, who gives life to everything,
> and of Christ Jesus. (1 Timothy 6:11-13 NIV)*

FEMALE

> *Who can find a virtuous woman? for her price is far above rubies.
> (Proverbs 31:10 KJV)*

Virtuous is defined as a particular moral excellence.
Women: has the old phrase "save the best for last" ever
resonated in your mind? Have you ever wondered why God saved

---

22. Trey Chaney, "Simple Things."

you for the last of all His creation? God's purpose for creating man was to glorify Him in all things. In order to effectively do that, His plan included the sanctification brought on by the man-woman relationship. A woman completes a man. Woman was made from a man's rib, but every man is now made from a woman's womb. God's first action after creating the world was giving a man a virtuous woman who would support, help, and push him into his destiny. It's no wonder that after God created everything in the world, He took His time to create the intricate woman.

As men, we sit and ponder what we believe a virtuous woman should be. Any genuine, God-led man will say, "This type of woman should be of extraordinary character." Indeed, this is true. But as sinful creatures, both men and women are guilty of blinded eyes, succumbing to social norms and ideologies. Being a woman doesn't automatically mean you are virtuous. It is something women must work toward and aspire to be. The only way to achieve a virtuous character is to be one with Christ and live for Him alone—not the world.

If you look at social media, the woman with the most views but with no significant achievements is often the one who reveals the most skin. It is understandable why a woman would feel like she needs to show off her body, because she is constantly bombarded with the media's idealized view of perfection and validation. If we turn on any reality, sports, or local news channel, many times we see women wearing provocative clothing. For example: When the female meteorologist announces the forecast for the day, men may be struck by how her clothing accentuates her curves and they completely miss the warning that they need an umbrella for the inevitable downpour that will come midday. They are drawn to and distracted by the world's view of beauty and perfection, and they miss the important things.

Is this her fault for choosing a form-fitting dress? Is this society's fault for teaching us what we should find attractive? Is this man's fault for having a lustful, sinful nature? The fact that we have to even ask these questions is proof of how grossly blind we are. Society accepts the phrase "less is best" for women's apparel, but the Bible says otherwise:

> I also want the women to dress modestly, with decency and propriety,
> adorning themselves, not with elaborate hairstyles or gold or pearls

or expensive clothes, but with good deeds, appropriate for women who profess to worship God. (1 Timothy 2:9-10 NIV)

There is a commonality between these women and women today—trying to dress to impress. And while doing so may bring them plenty of attention, it does nothing for their walk with Christ. God is grieved when women lower their standards for status and material possessions. Usually, the same characteristics women use to improve their status wind up being their downfall. They end up with an identity crisis, as they try to elevate their worth based on their "effortless beauty" and social status and always come up short in some way—too fat/too thin, too much makeup, too many/too few muscles, hair is too straight/too frizzy, not enough followers on social media, and the list goes on.

Society teaches all women (like men) to care for the things of this world, but God clarifies the difference in cares based on a woman's marital status.

There is difference also between a wife and a virgin. The unmarried woman careth for the things of the Lord, that she may be holy both in body and in spirit: but she that is married careth for the things of the world, how she may please her husband. (1 Corinthians 7:34 KJV)

God's Word shows that being a single woman is in no way inferior to being a married woman. In fact, in some ways, being a single woman is better: a single woman can give her undivided attention to serving God, whereas a married woman's attention is divided among her husband, family, and God.

Some women believe that favor, brought about through status and material possessions, is the consummate lifestyle. We have likely heard the women's self-congratulatory praise report: "Girl, I am blessed and highly favored." But the Word of God says favor is deceitful, and when a woman brings reverence to the Lord, she will be praised. This means "her whole life is centered around honor and reverence for God, compassion for those in need and faithfulness and love toward her family."[23]

23. *Fire Bible*, Proverbs 31:30 note.

*Favour is deceitful, and beauty is vain: but a woman that feareth
the Lord, she shall be praised. (Proverbs 31:30 KJV)*

The Bible clearly states what should happen to a woman of
this quality.

*Honor her for all that her hands have done, and let her works
bring her praise at the city gate. (Proverbs 31:31 NIV)*

LOVE AND LUST

In my senior year of college, I began dating a young woman
who was in her final year of nursing school. She was also a model
and a member of the AKA sorority, and she had her own place.
She was about five-foot-four, 130 pounds, and "red bone."[24] I had
just purchased my Escalade and was looking to purchase a home.
Together, we were what society classified as a duel threat. The
underlying problem was both of us emphasized how society and
our peers viewed us. I was actually attracted to her because of her
provocative style of clothing, but when we became a couple, I didn't
like the attention she received. She was attracted to me because of
my material possessions, status, and outward appearance, but she
was insecure when I was away from home. The trust issues we had as
a result of this blinded view of a relationship destined us for failure.

Physical intimacy might have been the only force holding us
together. I am not sure if either of us made it to the "love" phase of
this relationship, but it was evident we were in the "lustful" phase.
We practically lived with each other, so intimacy was almost a daily
routine. We might have thought it was love, but we were deeply
blinded by lust.

A study done by Helen Fisher, an evolutionary biologist,
suggests that,

> People think love is a feeling or an emotion, but new
> neuroscience suggests that love ain't nothing but a
> brain thing. There are three intersecting brain systems
> that correspond to sex, romantic love, and long-term
> attachment. These three systems cover all facets of

24. This is slang for, "light-skinned with a nice figure."

love—romantic, parental, filial, platonic, and yes even lust. Sex drive is in the hypothalamus which is linked to pituitary glands which produce the hormone necessary to have sex.

She further states,

Romantic love is not an emotion, but a drive. Lust may be the simplest of the three hypothesized systems, an almost reflex-like process that keeps us getting busy. The connection to someone is a rewarding behavior, hence that ventral pallidum activation—it's nice to have someone to come home to. Somewhere in the middle is the romantic love system—connected to both lust and attachment. It hits on areas involved in attachment and lust as well as those implicated in rewarding process and learning. These systems work together, but it's also fair to say they don't often work together. So one might feel deep attachment to one partner, be in romantic love with another partner and be sexually attracted to many others. These overlap, but like a kaleidoscope, the patterns are different.[25]

This study shows why the love we think we feel might be overlapped lust. Many of us can attest that the reason we feel we are in love is actually because we are experiencing lust. And this is very much a societal norm for relationships. We can look around us and see that unmarried couples have no problem engaging in sexual intimacy. But this is not in God's design:

It is God's will that you should be sanctified: that you should avoid sexual immorality; that each of you should learn to control your own body in a way that is holy and honorable, not in passionate lust like the pagans, who do not know God; and that in this matter no one should wrong or take advantage of a brother or sister. The Lord will punish all those who commit such

25. Helen Fisher, *Anatomy of Love: A Natural History of Mating, Marriage, and Why We Stray* (New York: Ballantine Publishers, 1994). Helen Fisher is an evolutionary biologist at Rutgers University. Used with permission from Helen Fisher.

sins, as we told you and warned you before. For God did not call us to be impure, but to live a holy life. Therefore, anyone who rejects this instruction does not reject a human being but God, the very God who gives you his Holy Spirit. (1 Thessalonians 4:3-8 NIV)

God views sexual immorality as a direct rejection of Him. No matter how or what we believe we can gain in this life through sexual immorality, the Bible is clear that the Lord will punish these sins. It's important we understand the consequences that are coming to us because of the blinded guidance from society. In the end, our blinded choices will result in divine judgment.

Or do you not know that wrongdoers will not inherit the kingdom of God? Do not be deceived: Neither the sexually immoral nor idolaters nor adulterers nor men who have sex with men nor thieves nor the greedy nor drunkards nor slanderers nor swindlers will inherit the kingdom of God. (1 Corinthians 6:9-10 NIV)

Many people use sex as a tool for exchange of goods or other personal gratification. Some even believe that they are doing the other person a favor when they give themselves to them in a physical way.

We can assume when we give our bodies to each other we are doing others a favor. Is it possible to give another person our bodies as a favor? As if, we are committing a selfless act with our body. It's a given, sex is mutual or selfish. No matter what corruption a man is taught about the virtue of selflessness, sex is the most profoundly selfish of all acts, an act which we cannot perform for any motive but his own enjoyment.[26]

Know this, if someone is giving you their body in a context other than a marriage covenant, they want something in return—a relationship, personal gratification, a sense of power, feeling attractive. But it's impossible for us to believe that sex will give us everlasting joy. If God leads us down the path of marriage, we must all seek a husband or wife who reflects our true value—as imitators

---

26. Ayn Rand, *Atlas Shrugged.*

of Christ. Once we are certain of our own value, and Christ leads us to the person we are to marry (if marriage is in His plan for you), together as husband and wife you can feel complete in Him. (And if His plan for you is singleness, He will show you how to be complete in Him alone.) Completeness and ultimate joy is not something we can achieve on our own apart from God.

Women, do not be blinded by the glitter and glamour society places before you. A true man to celebrate is the man who loves God first. If he truly loves God, he will powerfully reflect God's image. When you see him, you will see God inside of him. A true man of God will carry you in his heart before he carries you to his bedroom.

We all fall short because of this blinded society. The identity crisis we have because of this blindness can be replaced with purposeful fulfillment. But first we must give our lives to God, accept His Son Jesus Christ, and repent. Once we do this, we are able to look to His Word to guide us, knowing full well that we are washed, sanctified, and justified by His blood.

> *And that is what some of you were. But you were washed, you were sanctified, you were justified in the name of the Lord Jesus Christ and by the Spirit of our God. (1 Corinthians 6:11 NIV)*

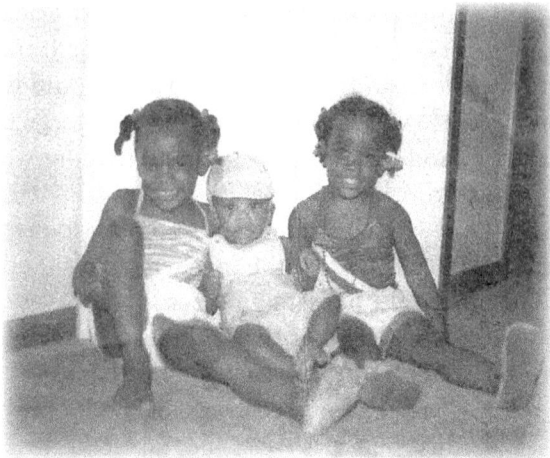

TREY (1) WITH OLDEST SISTER APRIL (LEFT) AND OTHER SISTER DAWN (RIGHT)

TREY AS A BABY AND FOUR YEARS OLD

1992: TREY PLAYING BASEBALL AT IRONDALE BASEBALL PARK

2004: NEWS
CLIPPING OF TREY
AS RUNNING BACK
IN UNIVERSITY
OF ALABAMA
BIRMINGHAM (UAB)
VS. TROY GAME

NEWS STAFF/MARK ALMOND

UAB running back Trey Chaney (20) finds running room against Troy last season. Chaney will likely not be available against Oklahoma on Saturday because of a right knee injury.

TREY IN UAB VS.
GEORGIA GAME

TREY IN UAB
VS. TENNESSEE
GAME

TREY GRADUATING FROM UNIVERSITY OF ALABAMA BIRMINGHAM WITH A DOUBLE DEGREE IN EXERCISE SCIENCE AND FITNESS LEADERSHIP (WITH PRESIDENT CAROL Z. GARRISON)

2015: TREY GRADUATING FROM TITUS BAPTIST SEMINARY SCHOOL WITH A DEGREE IN THEOLOGY (WITH PRESIDENT DENNIS FARR)

TREY'S EVANGELIST COMMISSIONING BY REV. CHRISTOPHER M. HAMLIN

2019: TREY'S FIRST SERMON: "THE AMAZING GRACE"

TREY SPEAKING AT AN EVENT

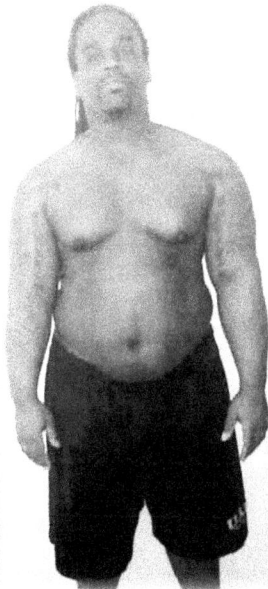

IN REMEMBRANCE OF ME

TREY BEFORE AND AFTER PRISON

2018: TREY'S FIRST SUNDAY AT
HIS CHURCH AFTER PRISON,
WITH PARENTS MANUEL AND
BONITA CHANEY

TREY AFTER CHURCH
WITH LANA

TREY WITH SYDNEY,
LANA'S DAUGHTER

GRAND OPENING FLYER FOR NEW GYM:
I AM LOVE FITNESS TRAINING CENTER

COACH TREY

I AM LOVE FITNESS ONLINE COACHES COURTNEY SHIELDS AND MARCUS "CHIP" SHEPHERD AT FIRST EVENT: "FAITH AND FORK FITNESS EVENT"

TREY IN THE GYM

TREY IN CROSSFIT
COMPETITION DOING
KIPPING PULL-UPS

I AM LOVE
TRAINERS
AND
COACHES,
OMAR,
ALEXIS, AND
TYE

I AM LOVE
CROSSFIT
COMPETITION
TEAM:
COURTNEY,
MAURI, AND AMY

7

EYE OPENER

Jesus stopped and called them. "What do you want me to do for you?" he asked. "Lord," they answered, "we want our sight." Jesus had compassion on them and touched their eyes. Immediately they received their sight and followed him. (Matthew 20:32-34 NIV)

E *ye opener* is defined as "something startling" or "surprising."[27] By far one of the greatest revelations we can ever have is to know God made us a certain way, and therefore we can accomplish a certain purpose. While there are many gifts, talents, and abilities inside all of us, God seeks out the supernatural things. In order for us to tap into this supernatural force, we must meet this supernatural God. Our supernatural God goes by the name, "I AM." No matter what we have gone through, what we are currently going through, or what we will go through, I AM will be right there with us to strengthen us through everything. Jesus said,

> *These things I have spoken unto you, that in me ye might have peace. In the world ye shall have tribulation: but be of good cheer; I have overcome the world. (John 16:33 KJV)*

This is confirmation that nothing can happen in this world that Jesus has not already defeated.

---

27. Merriam-Webster Dictionary, keyword: *eye opener.*

Are you wondering who exactly I AM is? I AM is the name God gave Himself as representation for whatever we need in our lives:

*Fear thou not; for **I am** with thee: be not dismayed; for **I am** thy God: I will strengthen thee; yea, I will help thee; yea, I will uphold thee with the right hand of my righteousness. (Isaiah 41:10 KJV)*

***I am** that bread of life. (John 6:48 KJV)*

*Jesus said unto her, **I am** the resurrection, and the life: he that believeth in me, though he were dead, yet shall he live. (John 11:25 KJV)*

*Now I tell you before it come, that, when it is come to pass, ye may believe that **I am** he. (John 13:19 KJV)*

*Jesus saith unto him, **I am** the way, the truth, and the life: no man cometh unto the Father, but by me. (John 14:6 KJV)*

*At that day ye shall know that **I am** in my Father, and ye in me, and I in you. (John 14:20 KJV)*

***I am** the true vine, and my Father is the husbandman. (John 15:1 KJV)*

***I am** the vine, ye are the branches: He that abideth in me, and I in him, the same bringeth forth much fruit: for without me ye can do nothing. (John 15:5 KJV)*

*They answered him, Jesus of Nazareth. Jesus saith unto them, **I am** he. And Judas also, which betrayed him, stood with them. (John 18:5 KJV)*

***I am** Alpha and Omega, the beginning and the ending, saith the Lord, which is, and which was, and which is to come, the Almighty. (Revelation 1:8 KJV)*

One of the most astonishing statements God makes in the Bible is found in the book of Exodus. Moses was keeping his father-in-law's flock of sheep. He led this flock to the backside of the desert and came to the mountain of God. All of a sudden, Moses saw a bush blazing with fire. Although the fire came from the bush, the bush wasn't being consumed by it. Moses was in awe and decided to take a closer look at the phenomenon before him. As he approached, the Lord God called out to him from the bush and said, "Moses, Moses" (Exodus 3:4 KJV). Notice what Moses' response was:

And he said, Here am I. (Exodus 3:4 KJV)

At this point, Moses had not received the glory God was about to manifest to him. Moses' introverted response, "Here am I," proved that he was uncertain about the potential he was about to release in the years ahead.

God went on to say,

I have surely seen the affliction of my people which are in Egypt, and have heard their cry. (Exodus 3:7 KJV)

In verse 8, He says,

*And **I am** come down to deliver them out of the hand of the Egyptians.*

God could have said, "I will come down" or "I have come down," but God purposely said, "*I am* come down." Moses, however, was still not certain about God's glory before him.

*And Moses said unto God, Who **I am**, that I should go unto Pharaoh, and that I should bring forth the children of Israel out of Egypt? And he said, Certainly I will be with thee; and this shall be a token unto thee, that I have sent thee: When thou hast brought forth the people out of Egypt, ye shall serve God upon this mountain. (Exodus 3:11-12 KJV)*

Moses still needed some clarification, so he asked the Lord,

Behold, when I come unto the children of Israel, and shall say unto them, The God of your fathers hath sent me unto you; and they shall say to me, What is his name? what shall I say unto them? (Exodus 3:13 KJV)

God responded in one of the most astonishing statements throughout the entire Bible:

I AM THAT I AM: and he said, Thus shalt thou say unto the children of Israel, I AM hath sent me unto you. (Exodus 3:14 KJV)

God revealed to Moses, "I AM whatever you need me to be, however you need me to be, whenever you need me to be." This same promise God offers to us. He promises to be our . . .

- Provider, "Jireh" (Genesis 22:14)
- Healer, "Rapha" (Exodus 15:26)
- Banner, "Nissi" (Exodus 17:15)
- Sanctifier, "Mikaddesh" (Leviticus 20:8; Ezekiel 37:28)
- Peacemaker, "Shalom" (Judges 6:24)
- God, "Elohim" (Genesis 2:4; Psalm 59:5)
- Righteousness, "Tsidkenu" (Jeremiah 33:16)
- Shepherd, "Rohi" (Psalm 23:1)
- Creator, "Elohim" (Genesis 17:7; Jeremiah 31:33)
- Lord, "Adonai" (Genesis 15:2; Judges 6:15)
- God Almighty, "El Shaddai" (Genesis 49:24; Psalm 132:2, 5)
- Lord is there, "Shammah" (Ezekiel 48:35)
- Strong God, "Eloah" (Genesis 7:1; Isaiah 9:6)
- Lord of hosts, "Sabaoth" (Isaiah 1:24; Psalm 46:7)
- Most High God, "El Elyon" (Deuteronomy 26:19)
- Everlasting God, "El-Olam" (Psalm 90:1-3)
- Mighty God, "El-Gibhor" (Isaiah 9; Revelation 19:15)

Finally, we have the name I AM, "Yahweh" (Exodus 3:14; Deuteronomy 6:4; Daniel 9:14), which translates to "LORD." This revelation of the name is first given to Moses in Exodus 3:14: "I AM THAT I AM."

What we must know and understand is that the most powerful name of all is the name of Jesus.

> Therefore God exalted him to the highest place and gave him the name that is above every name, that at the name of Jesus every knee should bow, in heaven and on earth and under the earth, and every tongue acknowledge that Jesus Christ is Lord, to the glory of God the Father. *(Philippians 2:9-11 NIV)*

When the Jews tried to say that Jesus was demon-possessed in John 8, Jesus responded that if they believed Him and obeyed His Word, they would not see death. He also used the example of someone the Jews already believed in and said,

> *"Your father Abraham rejoiced at the thought of seeing my day; he saw it and was glad." (John 8:56 NIV)*

The Jews were disturbed by Jesus' statement and replied:

> *"You are not yet fifty years old," they said to him, "and you have seen Abraham!" (John 8:57 NIV)*

Then, this Supreme Being that was given the name above every name responded,

> *"Verily, verily, I say unto you, Before Abraham was, I am." (John 8:58 KJV)*

Now that we realize who I AM is, we must understand how He can and will open our eyes. The only way we can figure this out is to accept that our eyes are closed and our vision is blurred in the first place—or that we don't have our eyeglasses on. We must conclude that we have an eye stress or strain, we are wearing a blindfold, or we are totally blind. Then, I AM can be our Eye Opener.

In a physical sense, the greatest wish many ailing people have is a cure for their disorder. We can only imagine the joy they experience when their physician comes back with a report that they are fully healed. In Acts 3, Peter and John entered into the temple at the hour of prayer. A man lame from birth lay at the entrance, begging for money as people entered the temple; he was there every day. When Peter and John approached the temple, the man begged them for money. Peter looked straight at him and said, "Look at us!" (Acts 3:4 NIV). The lame man was stirred, so he looked at Peter and John closely. Peter continued,

"Silver or gold I do not have, but what I do have I give you. In the name of Jesus Christ of Nazareth, walk." Taking him by the right hand, he helped him up, and instantly the man's feet and ankles became strong. (Acts 3:6-7 NIV)

What the Bible describes next is the joy this man showed because of the physician's (I AM's) report:

He jumped to his feet and began to walk. Then he went with them into the temple courts, walking and jumping, and praising God. When all the people saw him walking and praising God, they recognized him as the same man who used to sit begging at the temple gate called Beautiful, and they were filled with wonder and amazement at what had happened to him. (Acts 3:8-10 NIV)

The very act that brought healing to this man is a demonstration of the healing Jesus wants to bring to us. It may not be a tangible, physical ailment, but we all live with a darkened, sin-enflamed heart that needs redemption. We need to accept Jesus as Lord and healer of our hearts, believe He died for our sins, and repent.

Peter saw the people's reaction to the miracle God performed through him, and he spoke to them:

By faith in the name of Jesus, this man whom you see and know was made strong. It is Jesus' name and the faith that comes through him that has completely healed him, as you can all see. (Acts 3:16 NIV)

As we can see, Peter transferred the praise for this miracle to Jesus Christ. Peter went on to tell the people what they must do to also receive Christ:

Repent ye therefore, and be converted, that your sins may be blotted out, when the times of refreshing shall come from the

presence of the Lord. And he shall send Jesus Christ, which before was preached unto you. (Acts 3:19-20 KJV)

Once we accept God's gift of salvation, He will come live inside of us—in the Person of the Holy Spirit, guiding us and providing us with the truth.

But when he, the Spirit of truth, comes, he will guide you into all the truth. He will not speak on his own; he will speak only what he hears, and he will tell you what is yet to come. (John 16:13 NIV)

This is an awesome feeling to know that the Holy Spirit lives inside of us once we accept Jesus. As Oliver Holmes wrote, "What lies behind us and what lies before us are small matters compared to what lies within us."[28] It brings our consciousness to a higher level when we think about the God who dwells inside us. And He tells us from the beginning of Creation that He has been inside us, meaning, He breathed His very breath into us when we were created. We are living souls today because of that breath. But the reason God lives inside of us now is because we have repented of our sins and turned from our wicked ways.

And the LORD God formed man of the dust of the ground, and breathed into his nostrils the breath of life; and man became a living soul. (Genesis 2:7 KJV)

And God said, Let us make man in our image, after our likeness: and let them have dominion over the fish of the sea, and over the fowl of the air, and over the cattle, and over all the earth, and over every creeping thing that creepeth upon the earth. So God created man in his own image, in the image of God created he him; male and female created he them. (Genesis 1:26-27 KJV)

One of the most amazing aspects of this gift God gives us as image bearers of Christ is our spirit and soul. We do not possess fangs, claws, or wings. Nor do we have any type of protection mechanisms in our bodies against physical predators. Yet we have

---

28. Henry Stanley Haskins, *Meditations in Wallstreet* (New York: Morrow and Company Publishers, 1940).

dominion over everything on the earth. This is because when God blew His breath into our nostrils, He gave us a living soul, a conscious reasoning processor that allows us to perceive, identify, and integrate the material world. The God we trust also gives our processor (soul) a purpose. This purpose is what all of us are searching for, and the answer is simple: we are trying to find our Eye Opener.

When we receive this Eye Opener, and when we learn to use it properly (i.e., listen and obey), we experience joy, spiritual pleasure, and complete contentment. We also receive unprecedented power through the Holy Spirit. I AM tells us that we have a power inside of us that is ready for release once we are fully committed to Him. In the book *When Power Meets Potential*, T. D. Jakes writes, "Our commitment to God is what actually positions us for our divine moment that calls forth our potential to strengthen and empower us to fulfill our divine purpose."[29] When we are totally committed to bringing glory to God, our ambitions conform to His, and our power is unleashed. And Jesus makes an extravagant promise to those who are committed to and believe in Him:

> *Verily, verily, I say unto you, He that believeth on me, the works that I do shall he do also; and greater works than these shall he do; because I go unto my Father. And whatsoever ye shall ask in my name, that will I do, that the Father may be glorified in the Son. If ye shall ask any thing in my name, I will do it. (John 14:12-14 KJV)*

Before I transferred to Millington Federal Prison Camp in Tennessee, I was imprisoned at Maxwell Federal Prison in Montgomery, Alabama. While I was there, I was an orderly in the mobile unit TV room. My counselor was really tough on me. No matter how hard I cleaned up the TV room, she would always find something for me to clean again. This became very frustrating for me. Then, one day, I saw on a bulletin board, "New Life with Christ Bible Study Class." This class was held on Tuesday mornings at about the same time I would have to report for work in the TV room. I thought to myself, *I should be able to get away from my supervisor for at least one day each week.*

Once I entered the class, a friend of mine introduced me to a seminary college course I could report to on Thursdays at the same

---

29. T. D. Jakes, *When Power Meets Potential.*

time. I signed up immediately. I was able to be off from the TV room two days a week and not have to deal with this counselor. This was all in God's plan of exposing me to His power.

While I was attending these classes, God did something to me—He opened my eyes. That moment was just as the definition described (*eye opener*). I was startled and surprised. Although I had come to faith in Christ before prison, my sanctification had been moving at a very uninspired pace. But as weeks passed by and I learned more and more in these classes, I began making conscious decisions to stop cursing, stop hanging with certain people, and most of all, dig deeper into His Word. The things God was exposing me to made me feel joy, spiritual pleasure, and contentment.

After two years, I received a theology degree, but most importantly, I tapped into the I AM presence inside of me. God had always been inside of me. The potential was always there. I just needed His power to meet my potential. God knew I needed to be pulled away from all the foolishness the world offered. He also knew He had to expose me fully to His will. I realized exposure was the key that unlocked my potential. And he used my counselor to help me get there.

Power gives potential exposure. (T. D. Jakes)

I had graduated from the University of Alabama Birmingham with a degree in exercise science and fitness leadership, but I never realized my fitness fortitude until I got to prison. Maxwell started a program where inmates could study and become certified personal trainers (CPT)—accredited with the National Federation of Personal Trainers. So I decided to give it a shot. After much studying and months of preparation, I was able to obtain my CPT license in 2014. I hoped that once I was released, I could get a job as a personal trainer.

After serving time for almost three years at Maxwell, the prison officials decided to take away the weight pile from the workout facility. I was very distraught about this, as this particular portion of the facility had become a safe haven for me—a place for me to really focus my mind and strengthen my body . . . and also pass time. I knew God wanted me to come to Him about anything, even something as small as a weight pile. So I asked Him, "Why would you do this, knowing I used my workouts as a catalyst to make my time pass faster?"

I AM responded, *Because your time here is up. I need you somewhere else so I can prepare you for what I have in store for you.*

I didn't know what to make of this. I tried transferring to Arizona to be close to my sister, but that request was denied. Then I found out I was being sent to Millington Federal Prison Camp. I figured I would go there, serve my last couple of years, and be released home. But this wasn't God's plan.

> *For I know the thoughts that I think toward you, saith the LORD, thoughts of peace, and not of evil, to give you an expected end. (Jeremiah 29:11 KJV)*

Once I arrived at Millington Camp, I discovered on day one that the camp had a weight pile, an inmate-led Bible study, and sermons. This camp also allowed inmates to take furloughs. Everything I could imagine (as far as prison goes) was here at this camp. I trusted God when He orchestrated my transfer from a camp that was an hour away from my hometown, where I had received visits every weekend from family and friends. Since arriving at Millington, I rarely got visits because I was nearly four hours away from home. But I continued to trust Him in total surrender and obedience, and God empowered me, prepared me, and opened my eyes to His plan for my life.

> *Now unto him that is able to do exceeding abundantly above all that we ask or think, according to the power that worketh in us, . . . (Ephesians 3:20 KJV)*

We all have to come to a place where we realize the mediocrity of a life without *hope*—a life without sought wisdom from the Creator. We serve a God who gives exceedingly and abundantly. We serve a *more than enough* God. When we turn it all over to Him, He will open our eyes to the wonders of life. Here is a beautiful, encouraging word from Charles R. Swindoll entitled, "Fix Your Eyes on the Lord":

> Until your eyes are fixed on the Lord, you will not be able to endure those days that go from bad to worse. Fix your eyes on the Lord! Do it first. Do it daily. Do it ten

thousand times. Do it constantly. When your schedule presses, when your prospects are thin, when your hope burns low, when people disappoint you, when events turn against you, when dreams die, when your heart breaks, look at the Lord, and keep on looking at him.

Who is he? He is Yahweh, the eternal I AM, the Sovereign Lord of the Universe. He cannot do what is unjust; it is against His nature. He has never lost control. He is always faithful. Changeless. All powerful. All knowing. Good. Compassionate. Gracious. Wise. Loving. Sovereign. Reliable. As Peter put it, "Lord, to whom shall we go? You have the words of eternal life" (John 6:68). He's right. There really is nowhere else to turn and no one else to turn to.[30]

It's time we all turn to I AM—The Eye Opener!

30. Taken from *Encouragement for Life: Words of Hope and Inspiration*, "Fix Your Eyes on the Lord," by Charles R. Swindoll © Copyright 2006 by Charles R. Swindoll. Used by permission of Zondervan. www.zondervan.com.

8

CLEAR VISION

And it shall come to pass afterward, that I will pour out my spirit upon all flesh; and your sons and your daughters shall prophesy, your old men shall dream dreams, your young men shall see visions. (Joel 2:28 KJV)

C *lear* is defined as "bright, luminous"; "untroubled, serene"; "clean, pure"; "easily heard, [seen, or understood]."[31] *Vision* is defined as something seen otherwise than by ordinary sight; a vivid picture created by the imagination; unusual wisdom in foreseeing what is going to happen.[32] If we join the two words (*clear* and *vision*), they could be defined thusly: *Clear vision* is a clean, pure, easily heard or seen understanding of something that is not seen by ordinary sight and is bright, luminous, serene, and vivid—created by the imagination. It is also untroubled, unusual wisdom that foresees what is going to happen.

Ever heard the phrase "imagination rules the nation?" It's true. Ever since Creation, God has been sending out His magnificent combination of *power* and *purpose* to all of His people. Those who accept Christ, believe on Him, and obey Him are the few who will realize the magnitude of this force. It is within all of us, but only a few of us will ever learn how to use it. It can be classified as unused potential, but many of us know it as *faith*.

---

31. Merriam-Webster Dictionary, keyword: *clear*.
32. Merriam-Webster Dictionary, keyword: *vision*.

God allows us to take our visions and make them clear through the lens of faith. Before we were saved, we didn't understand this ability; but through our salvation, God has cleared the path for this faith, which is inside us. Before we allow God into our vision, our faith is dormant. Many people believe that we receive this faith through some magical premonition God sends us. However, God instilled faith in us when we were created.

> *For I say, through the grace given unto me, to every man that is among you, not to think of himself more highly than he ought to think; but to think soberly, according as God hath dealt to every man the measure of faith. (Romans 12:3 KJV)*

When Christ makes our faith real through salvation, our imaginations become active and powerful. He uses our faith to reveal Himself more and more in our lives.

> *Because that which may be known of God is manifest in them; for God hath shewed it unto them.*
>
> *For the invisible things of him from the creation of the world are clearly seen, being understood by the things that are made, even his eternal power and Godhead; so that they are without excuse. (Romans 1:19-20 KJV)*

All of the invisible things in our minds come into fruition with God. They begin to manifest in our aspirations, our actions, our thoughts—and God will allow some of them to become a reality for us.

So what exactly is faith? The Bible defines it as "the substance of things hoped for, the evidence of things not seen" (Hebrews 11:1 KJV). Faith is the evidence of whatever we're looking for God to give us. It is complete trust in God. Faith does not base its hope on visible circumstances but on a confidence in God. Faith allows us to do things when we can't see the full picture. The late Dr. Martin Luther King, Jr. said, "Take the first step in faith, you don't have to see the whole staircase. Just take the first step."[33]

---

33. This quote is credited to Martin Luther King, Jr. The earliest evidence of this quote appeared in the *Cleveland Plain Dealer* in 1986. https://quoteinvestigator.com/2019/04/18/staircase/.

Many times we simply must act on this clear vision of faith. We must believe God in the spirit before there's a manifestation of substance in the physical. Faith is often hard because we quickly realize that God's timing is not like ours. But we should not forget that God has a different concept of time.

> *But, beloved, be not ignorant of this one thing, that one day is with the Lord as a thousand years, and a thousand years as one day. (2 Peter 3:8 KJV)*

It's understandable why this may be hard to digest. *How can we ever have any understanding of timing when our days don't mean the same thing?* Well, this question is valid when we only think about physical time and space. But we need to also look to the spiritual realm. God dwells in the spiritual world. We are in the physical world. When we ask God for something in the spirit—in His will—the manifestation process begins in the spiritual world. We may not see it realized until we can view it in our physical world. With this in mind, time is on our side! Quantum physics state, "Everything is happening simultaneously." That means once we accept God's view on time, whatever we want in God's will already exists to us. Albert Einstein said, "Time is just an illusion." This means it takes no time for God to manifest what we are seeking Him for. "Any time delay we experience is due to our delay in getting to a place of believing, knowing and feeling that we already have it."[34]

It's time we start completely trusting God with our clear vision of faith. We must act on what we are believing God for. Faith requires action!

> *In the same way, faith by itself, if it is not accompanied by action, is dead. But someone will say, "You have faith; I have deeds." Show me your faith without deeds, and I will show you my faith by my deeds. (James 2:17-18 NIV)*

Prison is a tough environment to endure. But, as time passed, it became the best environment for me to realize how faith works. It secluded me away from the pull of the outside world. In prison, I was able to conquer my greatest obstacle: I was able to understand

---

34. Rhonda Byrne, *The Secret* (NY: Atria Books, 2006).

my purpose for my life. While in my wilderness season, I used my faith to make some difficult choices for my life spiritually, mentally, emotionally, and physically. Let me break down these lifestyle choices in four groups.

SPIRITUAL

I decided that out of the 1,440 minutes in a day, I would give I AM at the very least 120 of those for study, worship, meditation, and prayer. I also decided I must establish a lifestyle of fasting. The Bible says we should fast and pray. Every last Sunday of the month, I fast for twenty-four hours or longer.

I began outlining the Bible in CliffsNotes® form as well. I plan to publish this at a later date.

I joined the choir, teach Sunday school, and give the sermon some Sundays each month. I also started to play the drums in the Sunday band. I attended Bible study Monday and Wednesday nights. I wholeheartedly made the choice to give my life over to Christ, fully. No matter what I had going on, Christ would get my first and very best.

And whatsoever ye do, do it heartily, as to the Lord, and not unto men. (Colossians 3:23 KJV)

MENTAL

My mental fortitude became the strongest gift that God cultivated in me. I stopped cursing, I stopped hanging around worldly-led people, and I decided to stop watching TV. I began to read as much as I could, and I really loved it! As the Bible says,

Study to shew thyself approved unto God, a workman that needeth not to be ashamed, rightly dividing the word of truth. (2 Timothy 2:15 KJV)

I truly believe God was not just concerned with reading and knowing the Bible—although that is certainly the most important thing. I believe He desires for us to understand the value of knowledge; that, to do great things for God's kingdom, we need to acquire as much knowledge as we can through reading and experience. Dr. Ben Carson quotes the following in his book, *Think Big*:

> *Every man who knows how to read has it in his power to magnify himself, to multiply the ways in which he exists, to make his life full, significant and interesting. (Aldous Hurley)*

> *Education is the best provision for old age. (Aristotle)*

> *Knowledge is power. (Francis Bacon)* [35]

After reading Dr. Carson's book, it saddened me to realize I had just been getting by my whole life. I only read books when I was required to for tests in school. So while in prison, I started reading more. I came across an article by Berteau Joisil entitled, "'They Are Still Our Slaves'—A White Man's Perspective on Black People." Here is one of the highlights:

> We can continue to reap profits from the Blacks without the effort of physical slavery. Look at the current methods of containment that they use on themselves: IGNORANCE, GREED, and SELFISHNESS.

While I will not quote the full article in this book, I will say this article alone ignited a fire inside me to never allow anyone to swindle me because of my ignorance. The article ended with this message:

> Yes, we will continue to contain them as long as they refuse to read, continue to buy anything they want, and keep thinking they are "helping" their communities by paying dues to organizations which do little other than hold lavish conventions in our hotels. By the way, don't worry about any of them reading this letter, remember, 'THEY DON'T READ!!!![36]

---

35. Taken from *Think Big* by Ben Carson. Copyright © 2009 by Ben Carson. Used by permission of Zondervan. www.zondervan.com.

36. Berteau Joisil, "'They Are Still Our Slaves'—A White Man's Perspective on Black People," from *Dream Builders, Dream Killers: Voice of an Immigrant from Haiti* (Bloomington, IN: Xlibris Corporation, 2010).

Here a few quotes that I like that relate to the topic of reading:

If we make every attempt to increase our knowledge in order to use it for human good, it will make a difference in us and in our world. (Ben Carson)[37]

If we commit ourselves to reading, thus increasing our knowledge, only God limits how far we can go in this world. (Ben Carson)[38]

The essence of knowledge is having it to use it. (Confucius)

I do not know the exact number, but I am sure that in my four years (so far) in prison I have read more than three hundred books. I also read magazines and news articles, which are just as engaging as books. I love this quote about the mind:

Remember, remember the body can only go where the mind has already been. (Unknown)

EMOTIONAL

While I found my stay in federal prison to be quite enhancing, my painful emotions from month one to month 48 (the month I am currently serving as I write this) subsided. The doubts and fears I dealt with when I first came into the system no longer plagued my mind. I came to realize that doubt and fear are not real. Those emotions are simply the thought that something could possibly happen. The majority of the time I think something frightening will happen, it doesn't.

With that being said, I decided to seek to understand the exact origin of emotions. I read an article suggesting that we could "deactivate our amygdala [in our brain], which involves generating emotions, especially fear."[39] This article pointed out that "if I named the emotion I could possibly transform it into an object of scrutiny, thereby disrupting its raw intensity." The article stated, "When

---

37. Ben Carson, *Gifted Hands* (Grand Rapids, MI: ZonderKids, 2014).

38. Ibid.

39. Mary Helen Immordino-Yang, *The Brain, Managing Emotions* (New York: W. W. Norton & Company, 2015).

people label feelings, this facilitates emotional regulation in the brain." Meaning, the more mindful I am of the emotion I am feeling, the better I can turn on this effective regulation circuit.

I was dealing with so much pain in the beginning of my prison term. When I started to engage in this emotion naming system, I began to feel better faster. I realized that God was going to help me through, but I still respected the phrase, "God helps those who help themselves" (although it is not biblically grounded). I decided I would never engage in a situation that would put me in a helpless state emotionally. This meant the cheating, scheming, and lying side of me was laid to rest.

I refuse to allow a poor choice or decision I make to bring me emotional suffering. And what I realized was that the way I was feeling was all from the poor choices I had made. I believe pain and suffering is senseless if it's something we control with our actions. Therefore the emotional side of me took on the serenity prayer model:

God grant me the serenity to accept the things I cannot change, the courage to change the things I can, and the wisdom to know the difference.[40]

God gave me the wisdom to make better life choices. Prison cultivated these decisions, and now I choose to be different!

PHYSICAL

Asceticism is defined as, "a religious doctrine that one can reach a higher spiritual state by rigorous self-discipline and self-denial."

When either man or woman shall separate themselves to vow a vow of a Nazarite, to separate themselves unto the LORD . . . (Numbers 6:2 KJV)

On December 14, 2014, I made a personal Nazarite vow to the Lord (see Numbers 6:1-21). This vow requires an individual to abstain from wine, wine vinegar, grapes, raisins, intoxicating liquors, and vinegar made from such substances, and to abstain from eating

40. Reinhold Niebuhr, "Serenity Prayer."

or drinking any substance that contains any trace of grapes. It also required me not to cut my hair.

A Nazarite was raised up by God himself in order that through their lifestyle they might demonstrate his highest standard of holiness, sanctity commitment in the people's presence. (Amos 2:11-12)[41]

Since I was in prison, staying away from wine or strong drink was simple. I have dreads, so I was never going to cut my hair, nor was I going to be in the vicinity of any unclean thing. But there was more to this vow I took. I know this vow was totally voluntary, but the issue I had when I saw Christians in my past was a problem. Before I was saved, I was struck by the hypocrisy of those who claimed to be Christians—their actions looked so worldly. With that in mind, I knew if I took this vow, I would value my Christian faith so much more than just words and no action. The first commitment I took was to rid myself of all unrighteousness. My mom would always say, "Filth in, filth out." So to keep my filth out, I kept my eyes from (almost all) TV. I knew the shows people watched were nothing but filth, so I decided that the only OK thing for me to watch was Alabama football.

I decided to clean up my language. I made a pact with a couple of guys, stating that if we said a curse word, we would have to do pushups or burpees. In my mind, we either cleaned it up or looked like the Hulk!

I went to a water-only diet for liquids. I ended up going to the hospital twice because I kept getting kidney stones! After the doctor ran some tests, she told me I had a low acidic level due to me only drinking water. She said I should drink one can of orange juice a week. So every Saturday morning after that, I drank my one can of orange juice. Since then, it's been three years since I've had a kidney stone.

Although my body was already healthy from working out, I changed my eating habits. I do not eat any sweets. I have learned through years of study that I can get my sugars through carbohydrate intake. I usually eat six to eight small meals a day. My favorite food is yogurt. I eat a lot of yogurt! Ever heard of probiotics? I realized that I needed food that would put me in the best position physically

---

41. *Fire Bible* Note Numbers 6:2

in order to work out three to five times a day. I love the statement by Ann Louise Gittleman, an American nutritionist who wrote the book *The Gut Flush Plan*:

> *We have to learn to fortify, flush and feed our digestive systems with the foods and supplements that allow them to work the way nature intended.*[42]

The next step to my vow and physical discipline was to be around people physically who enhanced me spiritually. This was no easy task in prison. I limited my time in the TV room or in gatherings that did not have a positive, God-honoring outlook. I joined a Gospel choir, became a leader in the church, and started teaching Sunday school classes. God made these things possible for me.

Presently, I am continuing to put these strict physical values into practice. This is not something I did for a little while and stopped. I have been committed to this since December 14, 2014, and I continue to be. Although my Nazarite vow ended in December 2016 (I trimmed my hair and I ate grapes), the values of keeping myself holy and presentable to God remain. As Alabama football coach Nick Saban said, "Don't practice enough until you get it right. Practice enough until you can't get it wrong."

I came to prison weighing 250 pounds, and now I weigh 180. Becoming a CPT really changed my life in prison. The only thing I will say about my workouts is this: if you can catch me on one of my five to seven workout days and work out with me, I will say, "You like dat!" Working out, for me, is a *have to*, a *must*. It's a lifestyle. I believe it is so important because of the stressors life throws at us. According to Robinson, Segal, and Smith,

> *Exercise has been proven to alleviate symptoms of clinical depression and a host of other mental issues.*[43]

Although I believe any type of exercise will lead to successful results when done correctly, after becoming a CPT, I quickly became

---

42. Ann Louise Gittleman, Ph.D., CNS, *The Gut Flush Plan* (London, United Kingdom: Penguin Publishing Group, 2009).

43. Lawrence Robinson, Ph.D., Jeanne Segal, and Melinda Smith, *The Mental Health Benefits of Exercise* (Santa Monica, CA: HelpGuide.org, 2018).

bored by every workout regimen I did. So I started looking into CrossFit and began living that lifestyle. CrossFit challenged me to be better. The Bible teaches that physical exercise is not as important as spiritual exercise; however, the Bible does not excuse us from the physical. I believe my involvement in CrossFit directly relates to how God has always challenged me. CrossFit: *Are you* fit *for the* cross? is the question I would ask myself. My purpose is to tell as many people about how to be fit for the cross as I can through the platform of being a CrossFit athlete.

> *For bodily exercise profiteth little: but godliness is profitable unto all things, having promise of the life that now is, and of that which is to come. (1 Timothy 4:8 KJV)*

> *Today, I know that physical training should have as much place in the curriculum as mental training. (Gandhi)*

Once we step into the clear vision of faith, we will be able to change our environment with our atmosphere. Think of it this way: the environment is all our surroundings; the atmosphere is the surrounding influence. No matter what happens in our lives, our clear vision of faith will allow us to change the situation. We can use our clear vision of faith in God to thrust us into our purpose.

> *Whatever you can do or dream you can, begin it. Boldness has genius, power and magic in it. (Goethe)*

> *I beseech you therefore, brethren, by the mercies of God, that ye present your bodies a living sacrifice, holy, acceptable unto God, which is your reasonable service. And be not conformed to this world: but be ye transformed by the renewing of your mind, that ye may prove what is that good, and acceptable, and perfect, will of God. (Romans 12:1-2 KJV)*

9

VISION AIDS

Therefore go and make disciples of all nations, baptizing them in the name of the Father and of the Son and of the Holy Spirit, and teaching them to obey everything I have commanded you. And surely I am with you always, to the very end of the age. (Matthew 28:19-20 NIV)

A*id* is defined as something provided that is "useful in achieving an end": an assist.[44]

To have a life of true happiness and fulfillment, we must have a "love your neighbor as yourself" attitude. How we affect the lives of others is what gives us unspeakable joy. The greatest commandments Jesus gave are found in Matthew 22:37-39 (NIV):

> *"Love the Lord your God with all your heart and with all your soul and with all your mind." This is the first and greatest commandment. And the second is like it: "Love your neighbor as yourself."*

Once we grasp the first part of this verse (love God with all our heart), we must move on to part two: we must love our neighbors like we love ourselves. There's no way we can love others and be a benefit to others if we do not first love God and love ourselves. When we love God completely, and we love others as we love ourselves, then

---

44. Merriam-Webster Dictionary, keyword: *aid.*

all our attitudes and actions will align with all the commands and standards of God's Word.

> *All the Law and the Prophets hang on these two commandments. (Matthew 22:40 NIV)*

> *For the entire law is fulfilled in keeping this one command: "Love your neighbor as yourself." (Galatians 5:14 NIV)*

Helping others has a way of giving us a boost at life. Living a life for Christ has always involved helping others in some way. As we lift others up, God always gives us that boost of energy and lifts *us* up. It is a replenishing feeling to know that God is helping us as we help others. We must learn to give this vision aid of love.

> *And this is love: that we walk in obedience to his commands. As you have heard from the beginning, his command is that you walk in love. (2 John 1:6 NIV)*

By giving us His Word, God gives us His manual on love and how to love others. "How accurately we perfect the love walk will determine how much of the perfect will of God we accomplish."[45] We must understand that everything we want to happen by faith will come from the vision aid of love.

> *Love is patient, love is kind. It does not envy, it does not boast, it is not proud. It does not dishonor others, it is not self-seeking, it is not easily angered, it keeps no record of wrongs. Love does not delight in evil but rejoices with the truth. It always protects, always trusts, always hopes, always perseveres.*

> *Love never fails. But where there are prophecies, they will cease; where there are tongues, they will be stilled; where there is knowledge, it will pass away. (1 Corinthians 13:4-8 NIV)*

On one of my first weekends in prison, when I first started serving my sentence, my father, Manuel Chaney Jr., came to visit me. I will never forget his words. He said, "Son, no one will remember

---

45. Gloria Copeland, *He Did It All For You* (Tulsa, OK: Harrison House Publishers, 2012).

how many touchdowns you scored or how many yards you ran in high school and college. They won't remember the degrees you have, the trophies you won, nor the plaques that hang on your walls. What they will remember is how you affected their lives with love. How are you showing love to others?"

From that day forward, I decided that, for the rest of my life, I would be a creature of love for others. If it's something I can do, I believe I must love others as a duty to God.

> *Now that you have purified yourselves by obeying the truth so that you have sincere love for each other, love one another deeply, from the heart. (1 Peter 1:22 NIV)*

In everything I did, I wanted it to show God's glory. Therefore, I decided to become a personal trainer and instruct fitness classes. I also started leading a Bible study in prison. I did all of these things to show the love of God to my fellow neighbors in prison.

> *Or whatever you do, do it all for the glory of God. (1 Corinthians 10:31 NIV)*

It felt so good to show the love of God to others. It made waking up every day in prison enjoyable. As Rhonda Byrne wrote in *The Secret*, "There is no greater power in the universe than the power of love."[46] I realized that everything I did in my past for my own selfish enjoyment had no comparison to the joy I felt in helping others. I came to understand how God designed us to exist for the betterment of Him and others. I also realized that the love of God that I show to others pushes me toward His plan and purpose for my life. As Margaret J. Wheatley said, "None of us exists independent of our relationships with others."[47]

Through this growth that happened in prison, the number one thing God placed on my heart to do before anything else is—pray. The power of prayer is what moves mountains in my life. It is the only action I have in my arsenal much of the time. Prayer works. And the mechanisms that make prayer work are faith and love. When I

---

46. Rhonda Byrne, *The Secret* (NY: Atria Books, 2006).

47. Margaret J. Wheatley, *Leadership and the New Science* (Oakland, CA: Berrett-Koehler Publishers, 2006).

couldn't call on my mother, father, or attorney, I could always call on God. By faith, I know God will be with me to hold my hand. This is the same attitude I have when dealing with others. When I see a brother in need on the compound, if there is nothing else I could do, I can always pray for him by faith, in love.

> *Therefore, as God's chosen people, holy and dearly loved, clothe yourselves with compassion, kindness, humility, gentleness and patience. Bear with each other and forgive one another if any of you has a grievance against someone. Forgive as the Lord forgave you. And over all these virtues put on love, which binds them all together in perfect unity. (Colossians 3:12-14 NIV)*

There will come times in life when we have to put on our vision aid of love and go in prayer for our brothers and sisters. Every single person will struggle in life. Some of us have been blinded by the wonders of this world. Once our eyes are opened, we will have to intercede on behalf of others. Many times we will need to fall on our knees and pray for others to finally see God's goodness as we do.

There's a story in the Bible that gives us a magnificent illustration of this vision aid. It's found in 2 Kings 6.

> *When the servant of the man of God got up and went out early the next morning, an army with horses and chariots had surrounded the city. "Oh no, my lord! What shall we do?" the servant asked.*
>
> *"Don't be afraid," the prophet answered. "Those who are with us are more than those who are with them."*
>
> *And Elisha prayed, "Open his eyes, Lord, so that he may see." Then the Lord opened the servant's eyes, and he looked and saw the hills full of horses and chariots of fire all around Elisha. (2 Kings 6:15-17 NIV)*

We have to intercede on behalf of others. To love others, we need to pray for them. "An Intercessor is one who comes in between God and those for whom he is praying."[48] Who are we sharing our vision aid of love with in prayer?

48. Derek Prince, *Secrets of a Prayer Warrior* (Ada, MI: Chosen Books, 2009).

AUTHOR'S AFTERWORD

Commit to the Lord whatever you do, and he will establish your plans.
(Proverbs 16:3 NIV)

N o matter what our plans are in the beginning, whether it's starting a new job, meeting our significant other's parents, or starting a new page on some social media site, the status quo is: we must make a good first impression. We have all heard, "First impressions mean everything," or "You only have one chance at a first impression." Thank God, this is not the sentiment I Am judges us by. Solomon put it this way:

> *Better is the end of a thing than the beginning thereof: and the patient in spirit is better than the proud in spirit. (Ecclesiastes 7:8 KJV)*

God cares what we do after the start. Even though we might fall short in the beginning, God cares how we finish. When we mess up, do we repent? When we're in the wrong, do we ask for forgiveness? Even though we start this life messed up and full of sin, we can finish in a different way. Paul explained it this way while he was serving time in prison:

> *Brethren, I count not myself to have apprehended: but this one thing I do, forgetting those things which are behind, and reaching forth unto those things which are before, I press toward the mark for the prize of the high calling of God in Christ Jesus. (Philippians 3:13-14 KJV)*

As I reflect on my life and how it brought me here, serving time in federal prison, I couldn't do myself any justice unless I finally said, *I'm sorry.* I'm sorry to the people I hurt and the families I took from. I'm sorry about the trust I once had that was lost. I'm sorry to my community, my city, and my state. I'm sorry to my country. Most of all, I am sorry to my Lord and Savior Jesus Christ. I asked God to forgive me, and now I am asking you.

As I've poured out my heart in this book, I ask that each of you reflect within yourselves and ask, *Am I right with God? Do I know if I am saved?* If you don't know the answer to those two questions and you want to know the answers, repeat this prayer:

My gracious and loving Father,

I come to you as humbled as I know how. I thank You, God, for being such a wonderful, awesome, perfect, loving God. I know I have made many mistakes in my life. I am a sinner in need of repentance. I also know You are a God of forgiveness. Today, right now, I ask You to forgive me, and I make a commitment to dedicate my life to You, to do Your will and follow Your plan and purpose for me. Help me, God, to understand that I can't change what has already happened, but I can change what will happen in my future. At this moment, I surrender all my bitterness, loneliness, and my low self-esteem to You. Father, I forgive all those who have hurt me and I forgive myself for my mistakes and the sins of the past.

I believe in the life, death, and resurrection of your Son, Jesus Christ. I believe that You sent Him to earth, to live a blameless life, so that He could take the penalty of sin upon His shoulders in the form of death so that we don't have to. I believe You raised Him back to life on the third day, and He now lives at Your right hand in heaven. Even though I have not seen these things, I believe them in faith through the gospel You have given to us in Your Word.

As you watch over us, please keep me safe from all danger, hurt, and harm. Help me, God, to start this day and every day with a new attitude and plenty of gratitude. God, use me to do your will. Bless me so I can be a blessing to others. Keep my mind and body strong and healthy so that I may help the weak. I also pray for those who are misjudged, misguided, misused, and misunderstood. I pray for those who do not know You intimately. I pray for those who don't believe. I thank You because I do believe. I pray for my family, that all have peace, joy, and love.

I pray for everyone who is saying this prayer—may they come to know there is no problem, no circumstance, and no situation that is too hard for You. For my God is greater than all of these. I pray the words of this prayer will be believed, received, and accepted into the hearts of every eye that sees them and every tongue that confesses them in the name of Jesus. For it is in Jesus' name I pray, Amen.

If you said this prayer and your heart believes it and desires to live it, God will reveal Himself to you. He will make you *right* before Him. He will take your life and lead you toward His purpose—all you need to do is let Him. In doing this, we must love Him and love others, and we must trust that He will do what is best for our lives. May we, as Christians, be a force in this world. May those who don't believe tremble and realize that we are unstoppable with God.

The dreamers of the day are dangerous men, for they may act their dream with open eyes, to make it possible.[49]

When we sit back and look up at the stars, we can see the possibilities staring right back at us—all that we can accomplish through God's power. We can look at God's beautiful creation and be pleased, knowing He had a purpose for our lives from the very beginning. When we need help and we can't find it, *stop looking horizontally, and look vertically.* That's when I AM opens our eyes!

The heavens declare the glory of God; the skies proclaim the work of his hands. (Psalms 19:1 NIV)

---

49. T. E. Lawrence, *Seven Pillars of Wisdom: A Triumph* (New York: Anchor, 1991).

ACKNOWLEDGMENTS

And let the peace of God rule in your hearts, to the which also ye are called in one body; and be ye thankful. (Colossians 3:15 KJV)

> *I can't choose my circumstances; I can't choose those who will support me. But I can appreciate people who care for me in my pain.*[50]

Throughout my prison term, I have had my highs and lows. But there is no way I could have ever made it this far without the people I mention here. I don't just want to thank you; I hold you in my heart, and I cherish you. These are the people who have affected my life, not just to make me a better citizen when I leave prison but to be a better person totally.

> *None of us exists independent of our relationships with others.*[51]

FAMILY AND FRIENDS

Mom and Dad: Mom: "Baby, don't be the weakest link." Dad: "You can always have a job as long as you will work." Parents: "Always love God and others." "Be a light, stay positive, and tell someone about Jesus." These things you instilled into me from birth. You guys never stopped believing in me and have always been with me no matter what. True husband, wife, and parents of God. I cherish you both so dearly. Love you, Mom and Dad.

Lana Baby Love: My heart, my baby, my all! From the first day we met in 2005, I always loved your amazing smile. Fast forward to

---

50. Cecil Murphy, *Making Sense When Life Doesn't* (Waterville, ME: Thorndike Press, 2012).

51. Wheatley, *Leadership and the New Science.*

present day, it seems we just couldn't get enough of each other. No matter if we were in touch or not, God always found a way to bring us back together. You are the true meaning of agape love, sacrificial love. You put four years of your life on hold to wait on me. I can't imagine the uncertainty, the hardships, but most of all, the patience you had to endure. In the book *Cherish* by Gary Thomas, he wrote, "Cherish means to go out of our way to notice someone, appreciate someone, honor someone, and hold someone. When we cherish someone, we take pleasure in thinking about them, and we want to showcase their excellence to others."[52] Baby, you have done all of this and more. I don't know what the future holds, but I know my life will involve bringing happiness to yours. When everyone turned their backs on me, you were there. When all my friends were too busy, you were there. When the world kept moving forward, you stopped yours for me. I will hold you in my heart until the last heartbeat. God knew exactly what He was doing when He sent me you. I'm in love with every part of your mind, body, and soul. Just hold on a little while longer, cause your Superman is almost home. My inamorata for life! #TeamUSForever.

Sydney Baby Love: My baby girl, I can't wait to get home to spend time with you. You're just a delight. Love you so much!

Jeff Greer: You were always there when I needed you. Promise to give my best. CrossFit, here we come. Love you, Unk!

Emmanuel Abercrombie: You are always there when I need you. Brothers for life. Love you, Bro.

Marcus Chip Shepherd: You have had my back since day one. Brothers for life. Love you, Bro.

Tiffany Jackson: Thank you for always being a true, real friend. Love you always.

Lebarron Marks: Thanks for always being there to capture the moment. Love you, Bro.

Brandon B.A.: My best friend and brother for life. Love you, Bro.

Kelvin Davis: It's so funny how we both went through the same process, but only God could have made things happen the way they did. I thank you for being the ear I could talk to when no one else understood. You have always remained positive no matter our situation. Thank you for introducing me to a life of a desire

52. Gary Thomas, *Cherish*, unabridged edition (Grand Rapids, MI: Zondervan on Brilliance Audio, 2017).

for knowledge. I am so thankful for your friendship and love. I am forever grateful for you and can't wait to catch back up to you in our new lives on that side of freedom. Love you, Bro.

Karla Ross: I can't explain how much I hold you in my heart. You believed in me from day one. You are truly an angel sent from heaven. Love you much. Forever grateful.

Uncle Rubin: I want to personally thank you (a successful writer for the *Birmingham Post-Herald, Birmingham News,* and other news organizations throughout your life) for taking the time to review/revise this book. Without your vision and guidance, this book would not have been able to come to fruition or completeness. I thank you for your prayers, love, and patience. I will be forever grateful. Love you, Unk!

April: My sister, thank you. You never stop believing in me. Love you, Sister.

Eugenio, Dawn, and Celona: Thank you, brother and sisters. You guys are always so encouraging. Love you much.

MAXWELL PRISON, MONTGOMERY ALABAMA

Staff

Case Manager M. Rowe: Thank you for your help in taking care of all my obligations when I served my time under your care. We talked about football, working out, and life as a whole. You were not just my case manager, but you really showed your love and care for people no matter their situation. I thank you, and I am forever grateful.

Education Specialist Mrs. A. Gilder: Thank you for seeing something in me to teach in your classrooms. I'll never forget all those times you called my name over the P. A. system. Most of the time, when you called it was just for workout and nutritional advice, but you cared enough to thrust me into preparation to teach. For that, I am forever grateful. Thank you!

Chaplain Douglas: Thank you for the talks, the guidance, and the caring attitude. I could always come and talk with you about Christ. For that I am forever grateful. Thank you.

President Dennis Farr, Titus Seminary College: Thank you for the love you show each and every day by offering Christ to incarcerated men all over the world. You are an example for all men to see. For that, I am forever grateful. Thank you!

Partners (Inside Prison, Maxwell)

(1) Deloach, (2) Bubba, (3) Tommie J., (4) Ford, (5) Tommy B., (6) Pop Robert R., (7) Shea, (8) Smooth, (9) Bookie, (10) George C., (11) Kevin T., (12) Big Mike, (13) Fabo, (14) Reggie: To all of you guys, I will be forever grateful for your love, your help, and every moment we shared. I will never forget. For that I am forever grateful. Thank you.

Kevin T.: Thank you for showing me how to be the best public speaker I could be. I'll never forget the book, *Attitude of Gratitude.*

MILLINGTON SATELLITE PRISON CAMP

Staff

Mrs. Brooks, Counselor: Thank you for pushing so hard for me to get my first furlough. Because of your help, I was able to solidify a future in CrossFit after I was released. Your care truly showed in your character. For that I am forever grateful. Thank you!

Mr. Carter, Counselor: Thank you for always making sure everything was done properly and timely and without any issues. You always went out of your way to help me. For that I am forever grateful. Thank you.

Rec. Officer P. Dillard: I don't even know where to start. You were like my uncle on the inside. I knew you were God's gift to us when I first met you. You were always positive, always excited, and only wanted to see us succeed. Thank you for the good times and the laughs. For that I am forever grateful. Thank you!

Case Manager E. Collier: Thank you so much for your help with my release and the encouragement you continued to give me after the result of my release date came back. You really have gone to bat for me even when so many said that you would not. Because of you,

I still feel my work and goals are reachable in everything that I do. For that I am forever grateful.

Case Manager Mrs. Williams: Thank you so much for helping me with my halfway house paperwork, even though I was not on your case load. You went above and beyond to help me, even though times did not call for it. You really do help guys all the time, and I am forever grateful for your help.

Food Service Supervisor T. Brooks: Thank you for believing in me even while being incarcerated in the BOP. You allowed me to come into food service and learn under you, and I had a good time while doing so. Because of you, I was able to stay strong with my nutrition and health. For that I am forever grateful.

Acting Unit Manager Mrs. Smallwood: Thank you for trying so hard to get me extra time for my release back into society. After you reviewed my case, you saw fit that I be a candidate for extra halfway house time. Thank you also for the talks we had in your office about the government and the plans for the BOP. It was really an eye opener. For that I will forever be grateful.

Unit Manager Johnny Williams: Thank you for giving me a chance. You sent me out on speaking engagements, allowed me to furlough for CrossFit sponsorships, and always wanted the best for us. The camp was different the day you left. We missed you so much. Thank you for the good times when times were tough. For that I am forever grateful. Thank you!

Camp Administrator Tonya Hawkins: Thank you for approving everything I needed. Because of you, everything I had when I left prison was possible. If every prison in America had you as its leader, guys would succeed. Why? Because you really do care. For that I am forever grateful. Thank you!

Partners (Inside Prison)

1. Saddiq: My brother forever. Thanks for always taking care of me.

2. Heath: Strongest man alive! Taught me everything about CrossFit.

3. Uncle Phil: Always was there for me. Love you, Unk.

4. Uncle Klondike

5. Silver Back Ced—Silly Ced

6. Nitty FuFu

7. The Wiley Brothers

8. Tay Tay

9. E. Z. E.: Baddest man on the planet with Achilles.

10. J Smooth

11. Peanut

12. Nate: My workout partner for life. Love you, Bro. Thank you.

13. J Mack: True brother. Always had my back. Love you, Bro.

14. Walt T.: You always wanted me to succeed. Thanks for wearing your mask and giving me space to study, read, and prepare for my future. Love you, Bro.

15. Killa Kane: Watch out for the man in the ceiling. Thanks, Bro.

16. Mr. Ward: Christian bro forever.

17. Bro. Mon: My mentor, bro in Christ. Thanks for believing in me and pushing me to always be the best. Love you, Bro.

18. Larry "Thunder" Thornton: You put your name, company, and all of your resources into me. I know God has His hands on your life. I can't even understand why God does the things He does. But, we will be friends forever. You're like another father. I am grateful for your friendship. Love you. Now pick dat weight up!

19. John "Bump" Ballard: "You Can't Rise Above the Company You Keep." There is not enough room on this page for me to thank you. You're my forever Ball Cap—consultant, advisor, and partner. You believed in me so much, I had to tell you to slow down. You're my personal angel God sent to me. For you, I will be forever thankful. Love you much.

20. Shane Gunn: The smartest man in the world behind a gadget. You always wanted me to succeed. Your brain is brilliant, but please stay out of 12 feet. I'm in 3 feet. Thank you for the discussions, help, and love. I will forever be thankful.

21. Steve "Editor in Chief" Simpson: Thank you for the talks, the discussions, and the love. This book wouldn't have happened without your expertise. For you, I am forever grateful. Thank you.

To all of you, I am forever grateful. See you all on that side of freedom. Love you all.

Yours truly,

Manuel Chaney 111 (Trey)

@TreyChaney_IAm
TeamIamLove@gmail.com

www.ingramcontent.com/pod-product-compliance
Lightning Source LLC
Chambersburg PA
CBHW052204090426
42741CB00010B/2403